61-247

update

update

By Fred Hartley

Fleming H. Revell Company
Old Tappan, New Jersey

Library of Congress Cataloging in Publication Data

Hartley, Fred.
    Update.

    1. Dating (Social customs)   2. Youth—Conduct of life.   3. Youth—Sexual behavior.
I. Title.
HQ801.H34   261.8'34'142   77-1763
ISBN 0-8007-0861-X

TO Sherry and the other kids
at the Village Church who taught me
that God really has something to say about *dating*.

Contents

update

1
Nothing Heavy—Just Brothers and Sisters

Do not rebuke an older man but exhort him as you would a father; treat younger men like brothers, older women like mothers, younger women like sisters, in all purity.

1 Timothy 5:1, 2

Why date? Have you ever considered why God wants His children—you and me—to date? Our boy-girl relationships are prompted by several things. The basic motivations for dating are: (1) sex, (2) status, (3) marriage, or (4) just plain old fun.

I would certainly have to confess I have dated for all these reasons and have made just about every mistake a person can make. I have hurt people and been hurt, frustrated, angry, and basically empty after most relationships. It was not until I met Sherry, my wife, that I learned what God has in mind as his standard of dating. I have made many phone calls requesting forgiveness, and my past is now forgiven and healed. I have skinned my spiritual knees a lot in the process. I have learned the hard way!

This chapter suggests a new way to date. I believe it is God's way—the biblical way. It might sound radical.

Well, it is radical! I doubt whether you have ever seen it, heard it suggested, or even dreamed of it. It is what a very traditional God had to say about a very untraditional method of "dating."

Paul suggested a healthy dating standard to his younger brother in Jesus. He told him to treat the girls "as sisters, and no more" (PHILLIPS). Now Timothy was no sexual pervert. He had the same sexual drives and faced the same peer pressures you and I do. If we take these words of Paul seriously we are going to date a lot differently than we would have normally.

Let's just imagine that Paul really meant what he said and consider dating from God's point of view.

The Sex Syndrome

In the Monday morning rush to class you can plan on overhearing the question, "Well, how much did you get off her?" Dating often degenerates into the "without a kiss on the first date it's been a total waste" mentality. If you were to look at the way the average person does things, you would conclude sex is a popular motive in dating. Clearly God intended something better.

I consider myself fortunate to have a sister, Alana, who is seven years older than myself. We have always gotten along very well. Therefore, when Paul says, "Treat younger women as sisters, and no more," I can relate. One thing a boy would never do with his sister is to have sex. This thought is so far from righteous, I have to force myself to even consider it. Likewise I should not even consider having any form of sex with my sister in the Lord. They are equally perverted.

Galatians 5:1 says "For freedom Christ has set us free: stand fast therefore, and do not submit again to a yoke of slavery." In dating there are all kinds of yokes we can slip over our necks. Sexual slavery is probably the worst yoke facing those in a boy-girl relationship. Second Peter 2 gives a good description of the fake freedom of the contemporary sexual liberation:

> With their high-sounding nonsense they use the sensual pull of the lower passions to attract those who were just on the point of cutting loose from their companions in evil. They promise them liberty. Liberty!— when they themselves are bound hand and foot to utter depravity. For a man is the slave of whatever masters him.
>
> 2 Peter 2:18, 19 PHILLIPS

This follows the words: "Their eyes cannot look at a woman without lust . . ." (PHILLIPS). Now that is slavery! The yoke of "sexual freedom."

Furthermore, sex is an area to flee during the days of youth. The Word of God clearly states, "So shun youthful passions, and aim at righteousness, faith, love and peace, along with those who call upon the Lord from a pure heart" (2 Timothy 2:22).

We will talk more about the dangers of sex later in the chapter "He Loves Me; He Lusts Me Not." Certainly in God's eyes, sex should not be a motive for dating.

The Status Syndrome

One of the greatest diseases that spreads in the hall-ways of junior and senior high school is peer pressure. It spreads very subtly, but feeds on everyone's pride. When I was growing up I caught a bad case of the disease and it almost crippled me.

One fall afternoon after a football game I was walking along with a girl, cracking a lot of jokes with the other players thinking I was the greatest thing since Groucho Marx. We got into our cars and drove off in different directions. After a few minutes of silence I realized the girl I was with had been staring at me. When I glanced over at her, she said, "You are different when you are with them than when you are alone." My mouth dropped as if I was getting ready to swallow a sword, but I swallowed something greater—my pride. I do not remember what happened next. I probably tried to deny it, but it was true. I was not myself when I was with them. In fact, the only reason I dated this girl was to build myself up in the eyes of other people.

As we mentioned before, Jesus Christ has set us free and it is foolish to submit to any form of yoke. Proverbs 29:25 reads, "The fear of man lays a snare, but he who trusts in the LORD is safe."

As we make our reputation the "almighty" thing, we are ensnared by what others think. Thus, popularity becomes a yoke.

One of the greatest characteristics of a family is *acceptance*. No one has to measure up to anyone else in order to be a part of it. Our hair does not have to be combed properly. We do not have to dress real hip and we do not have to say witty things. There is no one we need to impress in order to be a part of it. I am a Hartley not only when I am clever, handsome, smart, and a good athlete. I am a Hartley for only one reason: I was born a Hartley. Alana is my sister because she was born my sister, not because I won her respect.

One of the greatest characteristics of the family of God should also be acceptance. We should not strive to impress our brothers or sisters—merely accept them. "Treat the younger women as sisters, and no more."

The Marriage Syndrome—The Ultimate Mate

Throughout junior and senior high I was in search of the ultimate woman: the girl who was beautiful, shapely, wealthy, talkative, humorous, a spiritual giant, and a lot of fun. In fact, as I met a new girl, I would ask myself, "Is this *the* one?" I would date the girl constantly until I found something that would disqualify her from being the perfect girl; then it would be over. She would never see me again. I stopped dating girls for a number of worthless reasons. Either I did not like her perfume, her nagging mother, or her hairy legs.

Needless to say, the thought of marrying a sister in the Lord should be as far from our thoughts as marrying our own sister. I did not go looking for the perfect sister nor reject her when I found that she had faults. Alana was not my sister because I wanted her to be my sister, nor would she cease to be my sister if I did not want her as that. Similarly, our brothers and sisters in Jesus are

brothers and sisters and although we will have prefer-
ences, there is to be no rejection involved. "Treat
younger women like sisters, and no more."

This mentality of looking for the perfect person was
a yoke around my neck. It constantly led me from one
disappointment and unfulfillment to another. It
brought neither personal growth, satisfaction, nor last-
ing joy. I was in bondage to my search and was scarring
myself and others in my pursuit.

Not only do we look for the perfect girl (or the perfect boy) for the sake of satisfying ourselves, but many
have the notion that without being married we are
somehow incomplete—as if the marriage partner will
be the other half we have been looking for all our lives.
Being single, then, would be something less than whole
—something to grow out of. Anyone over twenty-five
years old without a life partner would be looked upon
as rather strange.

Paul came down hard on this misconception.

> I wish that all were as I myself am. But each has his
> own special gift from God, one of one kind and one of
> another. To the unmarried and the widows I say that
> it is well for them to remain single as I do.
>
>   1 Corinthians 7:7, 8

God makes singleness a sacred condition just as marriage is a sacred institution. It is a lie to say that a boy
or girl is incomplete until married. It is also a false and
unrighteous goal to go "husband hunting." How often

little girls, when asked what they are going to do in life, will respond, "I am going to get married and raise a family." There is no way you are going to find God's best in your life if you are looking for a husband. Paul again wrote, "Do not seek a wife." How plain can you get? He continued, "But if you should marry," indicating that it should come as a surprise to anyone. (*See* 1 Corinthians 7:27, 28.) If by being married, we can serve Jesus better, then *to our surprise,* He will bring "the one" across our path. But He could just as well not bring a mate for us. He might choose to bless us with the sacred condition of singleness.

God does not want His followers to spend their thoughts or energies over the "who, when, or where" of a marriage partner or even the ultimate mate. This is a vain and frustrating pursuit. As the Bible says, "The unmarried man is anxious about the affairs of the Lord, how to please the Lord" (1 Corinthians 7:32). We are to be followers of Jesus Christ, not followers of dates. We are to be seekers of the Kingdom, not seekers of girls or boys. We are told to treat the girls "like sisters, and no more."

The "I Am in Love With Life" Syndrome

It is very easy to be out every night of the week with a certain person, to go here and there and do this and that and have months slip away. I have spent many summers in the dating-for-fun routine.

Nearing the end of August, things were not the way they used to be with my summer romance. Judy and I had gone everywhere and done everything together—tennis, golf, traveling, going to parties, and so on, for the first two summer months. I was away for a couple of days' vacationing. When I got home there it was, a little white envelope with a brief note inside. I did not quite understand the message, or maybe I did not want to, so I phoned her. I said this and she said that and before I knew it I was left with a click and a dead receiver, wondering where my summer had gone. That was a painful moment because all those empty surface experiences left quite a vacuum underneath. The hot dogs at the beach and the train ride to Canada seemed like dreams.

Jesus warns us very clearly not to lay up for ourselves treasures on earth (*see* Matthew 6:19–21). In dating language Jesus is saying, "Do not lay up for yourselves good times on earth, where romances can grow cold, and I.D. bracelets can be returned, or where Don Juans can break in and steal affections. But lay up for yourselves good times in heaven. . . ."

Being a part of the fun routine is like being strapped to a merry-go-round. You keep doing the same things, seeing the same faces, and when it is all over you have not gone anywhere except around in circles. That is not freedom! That is bondage in a bad way.

Alana and I always had fun together, but we also did more than just have fun. When I was three years old I fell out of a rowboat into a pond and she swam out and saved me from drowning. Ten years later she had a boyfriend who had just broken up with her. I took his picture and put a marble through his forehead with a slingshot because I did not want to see her hurt in any way. If there was anything we could do to help each other we would do it. We did more together than simply have fun and games. We should do more than simply have fun and games with our sisters and brothers in Jesus, as well. From what I have said, it is quite obvious that I have been taking it for granted that a Christian will date only another Christian. At this point some will probably close the book and put it on the shelf along with a daily devotional or some other book they never look at. Well, that is too bad, but I can only tell the truth, the way I see it.

Non-Christians; to Date, or Not to Date

I imagine we have all heard a lot of teaching against dating non-Christians. This principle is rooted in the Mosaic Law, and the Israelites knew that foreign wives were forbidden (*see* Deuteronomy 7:3). Time after time the Jews disobeyed this commandment and thereby suffered the Judgment of God (*see* Ezra 10). It is also understood in the New Testament that a Christian is only to marry another Christian. For example, 1 Corinthians 7:39 says, "A wife is bound to her husband as long as he lives. If the husband dies, she is free to be married to whom she wishes, only in the Lord." "Only in the Lord" means only to a Christian.

Furthermore, two passages in Second Corinthians are often used to teach against marrying non-Christians.

Do not be mismated with unbelievers. For what partnership have righteousness and iniquity? Or what

fellowship has light with darkness? What accord has
Christ with Belial? Or what has a believer in common
with an unbeliever? . . . beloved, let us cleanse ourselves from every defilement of body and spirit, and
make holiness perfect in the fear of God.

2 Corinthians 6:14–16; 7:1

Although this passage refers primarily to Christians
worshiping with non-Christians, the principle applies
to joining ourselves with non-Christians in other ways,
such as in the marriage union.

The Word of God refers to a Christian as the temple
of the Holy Spirit (*see* 1 Corinthians 6:19). When we are
married we become one with our marriage partner (*see*
Ephesians 5:31). If we join ourselves and become one
with a person who does not have the Holy Spirit, our
temple becomes unholy and defiled in God's sight. For
this reason we are exhorted, "Therefore come out from
them, and be separate from them, says the Lord, and
touch nothing unclean . . ." (2 Corinthians 6:17). This has
been God's law since Moses and it shall remain God's
law.

Despite the fact that most of us understand this biblical principle, there will probably be some who will
tragically proceed to marry a non-Christian. Jill was one
such person.

Sherry and I knew her to be one of the more emotional kids in the youth group. After Easter vacation
everything with Jill was "Bob . . . Bob . . . Bob. . . ." At
the time we didn't think much of it. Two weeks later

she had an engagement ring on her finger and the word was out that she was engaged to a non-Christian. I could not believe it, so I went over to talk with her privately.

Jill and I talked for a while and I showed her in the Word where it teaches that Christians should not marry non-Christians. All she could say was, "Yeh, Fred, I know all that. But Bob won't have it any other way."

"Bob won't have it any other way? What about Jesus? Doesn't He have any say?"

"Fred, I know what God says, but it's too late. Things are all set."

Before I left that evening, I prayed with her. When I left she had tears in her eyes, but there was no change. On the way back home I asked myself, "Why was it too late?" Those words—"too late"—echoed in my brain.

Tragically, like many others, she allowed herself to get emotionally involved with a non-Christian. Even worse than that, she became physically involved. Despite the fact that she knew in her mind that the Word of God said it was wrong, she was both deceived and ensnared by her emotions.

I know that most Christians will go out with non-Christians at times, but their relationship can only grow in certain directions. Unfortunately, they will grow in the unrighteous areas we have already discussed and not in the way God intends. As we work our way through different aspects of dating, I hope the concept of dating only Christians will come into focus.

While dating, I led a few girls to Jesus, but they did not grow in Him at all until we broke up. It was always a bad situation. The girl would receive Jesus to please me; while we were dating she would pay more respect to me than to her Saviour. The fact was, it was an ego trip and I lacked true love for these girls. If I was really concerned for them I would have done what was best and made sure that they were being taught the Word by another sister. Agape love will place the other person's relationship with God above all else.

We have talked a lot about what brothers and sisters do *not* do together and we have seen what places yokes over our necks. Now let us take a look at what God intends for His children.

2
A Little Bit of God's Better Idea

> So shun youthful passion and aim at righteousness,
> faith, love, and peace, along with those who call upon
> the Lord from a pure heart.
>
> 2 Timothy 2:22

What do you get if you take all the other reasons for dating away? What would happen if you didn't date in order to have sex or gain popularity? Or what would happen if you didn't date in order to get married or just to have fun? You would give God a chance to show you a little bit of His better idea.

Jesus came to proclaim release to the captives (*see* Luke 4:18), and He desires to liberate the old musty, dead forms of dating. He desires to smash those meaningless and worldly counterfeits and replace them with Spirit-filled relationships.

Second Timothy 2:22 gives us some more dating advice. It starts out negatively, "So shun youthful passion. . . ." but proceeds to give us four things to aim for: righteousness, faith, love, and peace. Let us creatively consider these positive aspects of dating which Paul suggests.

Righteousness

Aiming for righteousness is the most fundamental idea in dating as well as the rest of life. When you are aiming for righteousness you desire God's best in the other person's life.

Sally cared for Brooks very much—maybe too much. She realized it and came to me for a little advice. As she walked into my office I could tell she was rather upset. I silently prayed and thanked God for the situation and asked Him for wisdom. She proceeded to tell me her problem. I paused, looked at her, and said, "Give him away."

She looked back at me as if to say, "No, you don't understand. I really like him."

So I repeated myself, "Yes, give him away. You see, anything special comes from God. If Brooks calls you, asks you out, or whatever, you can take it from God. If he doesn't, you'll take that from God, too. You won't have to worry about liking him too much this way. God knew you could not handle him yourself, so He wanted to make sure you realized who is in charge. If or when God develops any sort of relationship between you and Brooks, Jesus will still be Number One." I told her about placing Brooks on the altar just as Abraham placed Isaac.

It was not long until Sally caught on. She understood God's love to her now and she knew that even this puppy-love situation would work for her good and God's glory. She bowed her head and said, "Jesus, I love You. I thank You that You know what is best for me— even better than myself. I give Brooks to You. He is

Yours. Take him. He is better in Your hands than he is in mine." She gave Brooks to God, just as if she was giving Him a present. "Amen." She looked at me and smiled.

Sally left with her spirits soaring because she was a faithful girl putting Jesus first in her relationships—aiming at righteousness. She wanted God's way, not her own, in Brooks' life.

Sally and Brooks go to the same high school and have since been actively seeking to lead many friends to Jesus. They are giving their witness higher priority than their own friendship.

I should also say, I shared this principle of giving Jesus Number One priority with Sam, and for the first five months afterward he did not date at all. You might think that is strange, but during those months, God really purified him, teaching him self-acceptance, and he has since been used to lead friends to Jesus Christ. Sam was obedient in seeking righteousness first. Recently he told me that he has never been so free in his whole life. It started when he laid his dating life on the altar of God.

Another way to aim at righteousness is to read and study the Bible together. It provides righteous soil out of which a living, Christ-centered relationship can grow. When two people are affectionate towards one another there is a lot of extra energy. A study in God's Word can provide good protection to keep two such people pure. Psalms 119:9 says, "How can a young man keep his way pure? By guarding it according to thy word."

On the other hand, praying together needs to be

done prudently. I have heard of many relationships ruined because couples began praying together. What begins with a very naive, innocent prayer can digress into a deeply intimate and emotional situation which distracts one's focus on Jesus Christ and His righteousness.

Jordan was a great brother, and he was vitally used among young people in his high school. One of the girls came up to him after a club meeting with tears in her eyes and with a tremendous burden in her heart. She poured out her sorrows. She told of past sins and confessed it all to Jordan. He offered advice to her from the Word and then proceeded to pray with her. They prayed for quite a while and when they finished her burden was forgotten and they were both sharing the joy of the Lord.

For several weeks they continued praying together about this particular need and then just generally for each other. Soon, without really being aware of what had happened, they were emotionally involved with each other with very real feelings of "romance." They were not aware of what had happened until one night when they found themselves kissing one another following one of their prayer times. They did not let this continue, but it shocked them both to see what had happened in a very subtle way.

Praying creates a very deep intimacy between two people—particularly two people of the opposite sex. Very often praying exposes the deep thoughts of our hearts which only God should know. It is unrighteous to expose these feelings to others when they cannot be properly cared for. After Jordan had listened to this girl pour out her heart to him and then pray with him, he was exposing himself to a very difficult position. If he had called on a sister to counsel this girl it would have been better for both of them.

Praying with someone of the opposite sex should generally be limited to a group situation. If you are a boy, you will be protecting yourself from further temptations by avoiding the intimacy of praying with a girl. If you are a girl, be very suspicious of the motives of a boy who desires to pray with you, and be strong enough to suggest reading the Word of God instead. There are certain times when praying together can be a very spontaneous and righteous activity and when we would be quenching the Spirit not to pray, but it should not be used for a selfish motive, nor should it be a gooey emotional moment.

Faith

Aiming at faith does not come naturally. It usually requires a conscious effort. However, there are a number of ways that God intends us to exercise faith in dating. One way is to keep our parents as a higher priority than the person we're dating. It took me a long time to realize this, but my patient father (and Father) bore with me.

Between ten hours of yard work and one date every night, my time during the summer months was pretty well accounted for. As I strutted through the kitchen one evening in July, grabbing a piece of fried chicken,

I waved good-bye to my parents who sat at the table sipping their coffee. "Got a date with ——" I mumbled. As I neared the back door my dad replied in his subtle way, "Hey, Fred, can I *have* a *date* with you sometime?"

Whammo! I didn't know it was coming and it hit me hard. Here I had thought I was so spiritual, involved with the youth Bible Studies and dating a Christian girl, but my parents . . .? What about my parents? In fact, it was more like, "What parents?"

From that night on I was home for a couple of nights a week, not because they insisted on it, or because I felt like it (because I didn't feel like it). I stayed home because the Word of God speaks truth when it says:

My son, keep your father's commandment,
and forsake not your mother's teaching.
Bind them upon your heart always;
tie them about your neck.
When you walk, they will lead you;
when you lie down, they will watch over you;
and when you awake, they will talk with you.
For the commandment is a lamp and the teaching a light,
and the reproofs of discipline are the way of life. . . .

Proverbs 6:20–23

I stayed home because I had the faith that these words were true and that my parents were a higher priority in God's eyes than any girl could be. You ought to take your parents out on a date sometime. It might really surprise them.

Another way to aim at faith is through giving ministry a higher priority than dating. One of the best things you can do for yourself, as well as your dating life, is to affirm before God and others that the ministry that God has given you comes before dating. If this sounds weird to you, remember that Jesus promised to make you a fisher of men, not a dater of men. A dating relationship can be healthy only to the extent to which it is secondary to ministry.

It has been a joy for me recently to see a dozen or more boy-girl relationships transformed into something beautiful because these young people have placed serving Jesus before going out on dates. The people who come to me with worries, problems and anxieties about their dating lives are the ones who are out three nights a week to movies, parties, and so on, and who have no time for ministry.

Proverbs 29:18 says, "Where there is no vision, the people perish; but he that keepeth the law, happy is he" (KJV). This is exactly true in dating. The "vision" is the perspective of bringing Jesus Christ to a group of people, and this means having a ministry.

Earlier, I mentioned Sally, who placed Brooks on God's altar. (Now, I hope you don't think that Brooks is a "nothing." He is the starting quarterback and president of his class. He's a real Big Man on Campus. Sally's no slouch either. She is a model, Key Club sweetheart of southwest Florida, and a Homecoming attendant.) They both have a deep concern for each other, but since they have placed ministry ahead of seeing each other, their relationship has the freedom and creativity that God intended. Sally told me the other day, "I have so much faith, I wish there were more things to pray about." Why is this? Because she acted in faith by putting ministry first and then her faith grew by leaps and bounds. They now see each other a couple of times per week. They are independently praying for the same friends and actively seeking to bring them to Jesus. This is their senior year and they know that Jesus has a lot for them to do for Him. Brooks has told all but a few guys on the football team the Good News, and has seen some of them come to know Him personally. This is a little of what it is to aim at faith, and will be discussed further in the chapter "Now, Am I Ready to Date?"

Love

Aiming at love is where I failed for a long time. When I was on a date I was usually not very honest. I never wanted my real feelings to come through because I was afraid of being hurt. If I was mad, tired, worried, or jealous I would never let on. Also I was extremely covetous. I wanted more or less to own the girl. I wouldn't want her to go out with anyone else, see anyone else, or talk with anyone else. I wanted her to be obsessed with me. In contrast, love is open and honest.

A very practical way that love can show itself in a dating situation is to encourage one another to develop independently. The perfect symbol of the covetous relationship is the I.D. bracelet or some similar token. It is actually a handcuff, rather than a symbol of affection.

In fact the whole idea of a "date" is covetous. "I own you from seven-thirty till midnight."

I can remember many parties and dances where I became very angry because "my date" was spending too much time talking with some other guy. I can remember saying, "You came with me, in my car, and I paid your way, so you are my date." This mentality is so far from love!

While at Wheaton College I saw a relationship that was so open that it floored me. I was very close to Bill. In fact he introduced me to Sherry, my wife. We picked up Ellen one evening, and on the way to the restaurant I overheard him ask her, "Who were you out with last night?" After she told him, I waited for him to blow his cool and get angry. He didn't. I was in the front seat screaming inside, "Hit her, Bill! Hit her! Don't let her do that to you." But he didn't. In fact, I think that he even told her that she had good taste or something like that.

At the time I didn't realize that I was seeing love in action and it actually baffled me. Bill had a genuine interest in Ellen's life that went beyond the surface. He encouraged her to seek God's will for her own life. This even led her to a different college almost eight hours away and in an entirely different area of study from Bill's. As Bill's love for her grew, he didn't try to tie the strings tighter; his strings became looser. So often we can mistake covetousness for love, but Bill's attitude showed love because it was open.

Also, love is honest. It makes itself known, no matter what the cost. If it's tired, it doesn't act energetic. If it's scared, it doesn't act strong. Love is willing to pay the price of being itself.

If you put these characteristics of love together with a few others, you'll have a relationship where real growth can take place in both lives.

As two people get to know each other, they should suggest helpful projects to help one another grow in basic areas of their lives—perhaps where there are weaknesses. Gary and Joan were two such people. It was the beginning of the summer when they started seeing quite a bit of each other. Rather than simply spending a lot of time together, they constructed projects to help each other overcome problem areas in their lives.

Gary shared that he was having problems in the area of telling others about Jesus. Joan likewise presented Gary with the desperate situation of having put off a summer's worth of school projects until the last three weeks of August. They both went home, prayed, and came up with projects.

It didn't take Joan long to come up with one for Gary. She called him and said, "Hey, Gary, what do you want to do before you leave for school?"

"Oh, that's easy; I want to see you!"

"Okay," Joan replied. "Then, you have to tell fourteen people what Jesus did for them at the cross before you see me again."

Gary's jaw dropped. "Aw, come on," he exclaimed desperately.

"No. I insist."

Along with this stiff demand, Joan gave him a stack

of creative pamphlets which briefly express the Good News in a contemporary way. She told him that she'd be praying for him. A week later Gary was knocking on Joan's door. He had told fourteen people the Good News and God had gained victory in his life in the area of sharing his faith. This was only the beginning, and since then evangelism has become a way of life for Gary.

Joan lagged far behind in her independent study project, and if she didn't hurry she would get no college credit for her work. Gary pitched in and offered much creative support. He enlisted other people's help, got people praying for Joan and promised her one of his mom's exquisite Italian meals when they were through.

A few days before the fall session was to start they were seated around a table of chicken cacciatore, celebrating together.

These two could have spent the summer sunbathing and waterskiing. But there was one problem—they *loved* each other and that love was constructive in each of their lives.

Peace

Certainly by aiming at righteousness, faith, and love in the ways we have considered, we will also be aiming at peace. There are, however, unique methods that will be useful in aiming at peace.

Very soon after Sherry and I started going out together, we started a study in Ephesians. One night we got into a little tiff. Actually it started as a little tiff and snowballed into a rather big tiff. Before long her lower lip was curled up and I think I even heard her growl. She wouldn't say a word and neither would I. We exchanged ugly faces and furiously went our separate ways.

As I moped in my room I thought back over what had caused the argument and there was no way that I could remember. This didn't exactly strike me as funny at the time, but I sure felt foolish. It was past midnight when I opened my Bible to our next verse, "Be angry but do not sin; do not let the sun go down on your anger, and give no opportunity to the devil." I went on to read, "Let all bitterness and wrath and anger and clamor and slander be put away from you, with all malice, and be kind to one another, tenderhearted, forgiving one another, as God in Christ forgave you" (Ephesians 4:26, 27, 31, 32).

I walked straight to the phone, dialed, waited, and said, "Hey, Sher, whatever you do, don't go to sleep. Meet me in the lobby right away."

"What's wrong with you! It's nearly one o'clock and I was almost asleep."

We exchanged a few more niceties, but before long we were sitting on a couch hunched over Ephesians 4:26–32. Sherry was still wiping the sleep out of her eyes.

Independently we bowed and confessed our sinfulness. God taught us that night not to let the sun go down on our anger, to talk out the disagreements, and so to aim at peace.

The real key to peace is found in Ephesians 4:3: "Try

always to be led along together by the Holy Spirit, and so be at peace with one another" (LB). To have a relationship active and growing in Jesus is to have peace with one another. To spend time studying the Bible, holding each other to godly disciplines, and creating projects to overcome personal weaknesses is the greatest method of aiming at peace.

Aiming at peace is like putting the icing on a cake. It's the last thing to go on. It's the most noticeable, and it is the sweetest part. If there is unrighteousness in our relationship there is no way that we can expect to have peace. If we are not rooted in faith we will not have peace, and if we lack love we will not be at peace.

Jesus said, "Peace I leave with you; my peace I give to you; not as the world gives, do I give to you" (John 14:27). He also said ". . . In me you may have peace" (John 16:33). The peace of Christ is available to each of us in our relationships as we "let the peace of Christ rule in our hearts" (Colossians 3:15). What a joy it is to have the peace of Jesus ruling in our hearts rather than lust, pride, or a host of other demonic counterfeits! When Jesus said that His peace is not like the world's, He meant that it doesn't depend on people or things or circumstances.

Jesus-peace doesn't crack when your "date" starts talking with some other person. Jesus-peace doesn't quit when you haven't seen your "boyfriend" for three weeks and you don't know why. Jesus-peace doesn't stop when you wake up the Saturday morning before the "big date" with a big red zit on your nose. People-peace depends on friends or things or outward circumstances and appearances. Jesus-peace is based on an intimate relationship with the Man. We can have His peace to rule our whole lives and this includes our dating lives. Are you willing to let the peace of Christ rule in your dating life?

It's really easy. Get on your knees and say, "Jesus, I give You my dating life. I lay it all right on Your altar. I put You first. I realize that there are both benefits as well as dangers in dating. I have a lot to learn, so teach me. I purpose in my heart to walk in Your steps every time dating presents itself. I will not go out unless I am sure that my relationship with You will benefit by the experience. Hallelujah!" Go ahead and lay your dating life on the altar of God. Do it now!

"Along With Those Who Call Upon the Lord From a Pure Heart"

The Bible makes it very clear that we as disciples of Christ are not only expected to date Christians, but we are to date Christians with pure hearts. No one is able to aim at righteousness while dating a person with a lustful spirit, and don't think that you are the exception.

What do I mean by lustful spirit? There are several ways to recognize a lustful spirit. Very briefly, the following characteristics can be used to identify such a spirit in a person: rebellious towards parents, highly critical (particularly towards those in authority), independent, guilty, frustrated, jesting, always making light of the situation, mocking the things of God, or questioning God's existence. It would therefore be wise not to date people possessing these qualities. As the Bible says, "Bad company ruins good morals" (1 Corinthians 15:33).

Another way of saying, "Along with those who call upon the Lord from a pure heart," would be to say, "Along with those who would creatively seek God with you in aiming at righteousness, faith, love and peace."

Gloria came to see me a couple of months ago about the "Christian guy" she was going out with. I asked her his name and as soon as I heard it my stomach had an unfavorable reaction. It would not have been righteous for me to say anything negative so I asked her some questions.

"How long have you known him?"

"Not very long."

"What do you like to do on dates?"

"Aw, go to Bible studies, have fun, you know. . . ."

"Gloria, what does he like to do?"

"Well, he likes to go to the Bible studies, too. But, then he doesn't like to do much else. We always just kind of sit around. He likes to be alone a lot."

I stopped her there and asked her, "Have you ever considered why God wants His children—you and me —to date?"

There was a long pause. "No, Fred. I guess I haven't."

"Well, have you ever considered what the advantages and disadvantages of dating are?"

"No. I haven't. What do you mean?"

I'm glad you asked, I said to myself. So, I proceeded to share some thoughts with her from 1 Timothy 5:1, 2: "Treat older men like fathers, younger men like brothers. . . ."

"Do you have a brother?" I knew she did.

"Yes."

"Well, let's just think how you would act with him." We looked at all the negative implications by understanding that she wouldn't have sex, wouldn't be with him for status, certainly wouldn't marry him, and would do more than simply have fun.

"Would you mind if we looked at another verse?"

"No."

So I read, "So shun youthful passions and aim at righteousness . . ." (2 Timothy 2:22). We went on to consider some of the positive things for her to do with a boy.

I could tell that Gloria was receiving the instruction because she never took her eyes off me. Her mouth dropped further and further as I spoke, and every once in a while she would roll her eyes and lightly chuckle because of the truth of God's Word as the Spirit applied it to her life. After some more instruction I suggested, "I don't think God wants you to date him any longer."

Although I could see the Spirit working on her I never really expected her to be obedient. She had an independent and weak spirit and I really expected Satan to lie to her and tie her up in sin with this individual.

The following week I saw her. She was radiant. "How's things with Jesus?" I asked.

"Oh, wow! Wait until I tell you. Well, first of all, I broke up with ――― and since then God has really been at work in my life. Wow! I really thought that he was a Christian, the way he went out witnessing and to Bible studies and stuff, but his life is full of sin. I really care for him though. I wish there was something I could do, but I know that now isn't the time and I know that I'm not the one."

Gloria was right. She wasn't the one.

A week later, I talked with him for quite a while and that afternoon the Spirit really ministered to him. God told him from Jude to repent from sexual immorality, but to my knowledge he never has. I know that Jesus desires to set all men free from the yoke of dating slavery, but not all are willing.

Jesus said in Matthew 24:12, "And because wickedness is multiplied, most men's love will grow cold." These are the last days and wickedness is being multiplied. In the high schools and colleges across the globe sex is making slaves of men and women. Television, newsstands, and movie theaters are filled with impurities. Never has wickedness been so worldwide. The end is coming soon and Satan knows it. He has vomited demons of filth upon the earth, and many of our brothers and sisters who are now in love with Jesus will lose their affections because they will refuse to date God's way.

We have been warned in the previous chapter against dating non-Christians. However, the Word of God also warns us most severely not to fellowship with, or particularly date, immoral "Christians"—those who consistently don't call upon the Lord.

> I wrote to you in my letter not to associate with immoral men; not at all meaning the immoral of this world, or the greedy and robbers, or idolaters, since

then you would need to go out of the world. But rather
I wrote to you not to associate with any one who bears
the name of brother if he is guilty of immorality or
greed, or is an idolater, reviler, drunkard, or robber—
not even to eat with such a one. For what have I to do
with judging outsiders? Is it not those inside the
church whom you are to judge? God judges those outside. "Drive out the wicked person from among you."

1 Corinthians 5:9–13

This is what Gloria did. Realizing that she was dating an
immoral "Christian," she discontinued their relationship.

If you don't want to lose your love and zeal for Jesus,
you had better make sure that your dating life is in
order. It is either/or. Don't think that you can live for
Jesus all week long—except for Friday and Saturday
nights.

Right now get on your knees and tell Jesus where you
are in your dating situation. Tell Him all about your
past. Receive His forgiveness if that is necessary and tell
Jesus that you'll put Him first from now on. Actively
aim at righteousness, faith, love, and peace along with
those who call upon the Lord from a pure heart. Tell
Jesus that you will not date again until you understand
the advantages and disadvantages of dating.

Someday your eternal life may depend upon the decision you make right here.

3
A Look Into the Mirror

Woe to the man who fights with his Creator. Does the pot argue with its maker? Does the clay dispute with him who forms it, saying, "Stop, you're doing it wrong!" or the pot exclaim, "How clumsy can you be!"? Woe to the baby just being born who squalls to his father and mother, "Why have you produced me? Can't you do anything right at all?

Isaiah 45:9, 10 LB

Just about every date starts in front of the mirror. We check out the waves in our hair, the teeth, the eyes, the shirt, the shoes, and even the zit situation. The mirror is either our best friend or our worst critic. The girls look closely to see if they have lost a little here or added a little there. The guys check to see if they have grown a little taller or a little stronger. The funny thing is that we walk away thinking, "I like it" or "Oh, no!" Throughout high school we either grow to love what we see looking back at us every morning or we grow to hate it.

I do not care who you are; there is going to come a time when that mirror is going to say, "Oh, no!" This morning I went into the bathroom and looked at myself: "Oh, no!" A big red zit right on the end of my nose.

I know what a hassle it is always trying to be cool. What adds to the problem is that we and our friends are the world's greatest critics.

I can remember in the seventh grade on the way home from school on the bus some kid told me I had small ears. After I got off the bus, I went straight home and looked in the mirror. I stood there pulling at my ears and twisting them around trying to get a good look. I got out two mirrors so I could see sideways. From then on when I would see that kid I would not turn my head. Maybe that is why I always wanted to grow long hair. Two years later, while having a physical for football, I asked the doctor if I really had small ears. He responded, "No. What gave you that idea?" I told him that I didn't know.

We not only judge ourselves on the basis of our physical appearance, but in several other ways, such as our talents, our parents and where we live.

I know a guy, Gordon, who never did well in school because ever since first grade he had had the nickname, "Dumby." He would come walking down the hall and the kids would all sing some tune about "stupid Dumby." Everyone just expected him to fail and so did he. In sixth grade he walked into class the first day of school and he introduced himself to his teacher: "Hey, Teach, I'm Dumby." The teacher looked back with a smile, "No, you're not, you're Gordon." He tried to correct her. "Ah, Teach, you got it all wrong, I'm a dumby; just ask anybody." Well, that teacher never believed it, and that year she taught Gordon and the rest of his class that he was not so dumb. From then on he did very well in school and today he is a professor in a leading graduate school.

Have you ever been embarrassed for your friends to meet your parents? Every girl has to face this when a guy comes to pick her up.

Once I went to pick up a girl for the first time. I had no sooner pulled up and opened my car door than I saw her jumping two steps at a time down the stairway in front of her house. I looked at her with a questioning half smile and asked, "What's the hurry?" Then I heard from the screen door, "Oh. Is this Fred?" The girl stopped in her tracks, flushed, and rolled her eyes. The door opened and out stepped her dad. She just stood there with her back to him. I went up and introduced myself and we talked for a while. He said something about what a fine girl she was and how proud he was of her, and as we drove away she said, "Now do you see why I was in such a hurry?" I admit that the guy had an outdated sense of humor and his slipper socks and Perry Como sweater were not exactly hip, but what really turned me off was her lack of respect for him. She was insecure just because her dad was "old-fashioned."

Today in our country, more than any time this side of the Gold Rush, people are moving from one state to another. When a father is moved for business purposes the family follows along. I know a woman who has moved forty-nine times. Often because of divorce, kids are forced to move to a new part of the country as well. For these and other reasons a lot of teenagers are living where they do not want to live.

Lisa's father was transferred from Georgia to California, and for a year or two she made herself miserable and refused to reach out to others and make friends. She had lived in the country with horses and ponds and many close friends that she had to leave behind. There was a boyfriend whom she was forced to leave and this hurt her more than anything. She was bitter and deeply resented the fact that she had to tear up all her roots. It was not until a few years later that she was able to thank God for the move.

Now, all these illustrations have one very important similarity. All of the situations were controlled by God! God is the one who gave me my ears and who gave Gordon his ability to learn, who gave us our parents, and who placed Lisa in California. God is in control of all these areas. If we are to look in the mirror and say, "Oh, no!" it is like kicking God in the shins. God was our personal creator. Now this does not mean that if we have a pimple or weight problem we can live on Coke and candy bars. There are certain ways that we can affect or abuse what has been given to us, but basically we are God's handiwork. David was a very content person because he recognized that his appearance was prescribed by God:

> You made all the delicate, inner parts of my body, and knit them together in my mother's womb. Thank you for making me so wonderfully complex! It is amazing to think about. Your workmanship is marvelous— and how well I know it. You were there while I was being formed in utter seclusion! You saw me before I was born and scheduled each day of my life before I

began to breathe, every day was recorded in your
Book!

Psalms 139:13–16 LB

If we are ashamed of who our parents are, or if we
look at them and mock them, we are telling God that
He made a big mistake. We should not be embarrassed
to bring friends home to meet them, because they are
God-given.

If we are bitter or resentful because we have had to
move away from one part of the country to another,
being forced to leave our friends, we are bitter towards
God because God determines where we are to live.
David recognized this when he wrote, "You chart the
path ahead of me, and tell me where to stop and
rest" (Psalms 139:3 LB). David was often attacked by
enemies and he was forced to live in worse conditions
than we are just because we're in some new school dis-
trict.

If we are resentful because we are lacking in abilities,
we are resentful toward God, because it is He who has
given us our abilities and has kept other abilities from
us. Even Moses had problems in this area. He thought
that he was stupid and had no ability to communicate.
When God asked Moses to be his mouthpiece, Moses
told God He had the wrong man. But God replied,
"Who has made man's mouth? Who makes him dumb,
or deaf, or seeing, or blind? Is it not I, the LORD? Now
therefore go, and I will be with your mouth and teach
you what you shall speak" (Exodus 4:11, 12). God was

telling Moses the same thing that he is telling us: "I made you. Now accept yourself." It seems that perhaps Jesus' disciples had a problem accepting themselves and he asked them, "And which one of you by taking thought can add one cubit unto his stature?" (Matthew 6:27 KJV). He was saying, "God made you. Now accept yourself."

If, when we look at our lives, we become embarrassed or resentful our dating relationships will never get off the ground. This is how it works. When you are with a friend, whether you realize it or not, your opinion of yourself is communicated to that other person. If you are ashamed of that zit on your nose, or your parents sitting inside the door, or perhaps your inability to play the guitar, you will communicate, "Don't get too close because I'm really not worth knowing." If, however, you have accepted yourself and love yourself, you will communicate, "Get as close as you want; I'm worth knowing," or "Accept me, because I've accepted myself." Once we are at peace with who we are, we can reach out to others and show concern for them. But when we are not pleased with ourselves we dwell on our problem areas and have to spend time compensating for our deficiencies.

Each one of us would love to see ourselves as we really are. The problem is we are always listening to what others think of us and we judge ourselves on the basis of their opinions. How do you view yourself?

MISS TERRIBLE   **YOU**   **MISS TERRIFIC**

If we are to judge ourselves on the basis of these four criteria, we will most likely either see ourselves as Miss Terrible or Miss Terrific. In fact we will probably vacillate between the two. One day we will be beautiful and later the same week we will be a jerk. If we continue to judge ourselves according to these four areas we will always be deceived. There is only one way to rest securely in the middle and actually see ourselves as we are. We must recognize that it is man who looks on the outward appearance but God looks on the heart (*see* 1 Samuel 16:7). Unfortunately, we live in a world that is hung up on outward appearances and this value system is almost engraved into us.

The year and model of our ten-speed, the length of our hair, how much our parents let us get away with, and how well we play the guitar all go along with the world's value system. But we, as Christians, have no right using the world's scales to decide what is cool and what we are going to pursue. We have God's value system to judge life by—not what is external, but what is internal. God does not want us running around judging ourselves or others according to what is external—hair, parents, or the ability to play the guitar—because these are all God-given. What is God-given is what He wants us to accept.

A good way to figure out if we have accepted ourselves or not is to ask the question, "What could I change about myself if I had the power to do it?" Right now think in these four areas: (1) What you look like. (2) Your abilities. (3) Your parents. (4) Where you live. List a few things that you would like to change. (Just imagine for the moment that you are God and have the power to make the changes.)

1.

2.

3.

4.

5.

Do you realize that each of those things which you would like to change about yourself is a part of your life for a special reason? God created each of us the way He did so that no two of us would be alike and that each of us could represent Him to others in a unique way. There is only one God and not any of us can change the way we are. Before God then we need to recognize that we have been ungrateful for the person He created.

One afternoon I spent two hours in Illinois talking with Josh about his life. He told me about a lot of things but we were not getting anywhere. Then I asked him, "Have you ever been hurt deeply?" He replied, "Yeah, how did you know?" He proceeded to tell me about his father, who had died of cancer when Josh was fourteen. Ever since then, he said, his personality had changed and he did not even enjoy being around people any more. That hurt had become like a splinter in his heart which built up a lot of bitterness around it.

That afternoon he opened his heart to God's love and grace and removed that splinter of bitterness. A week later I was walking along and over my shoulder I heard, "Praise the Lord, brother." I turned to see Josh, who proceeded to tell me that in the last five years his heart had been full of hate, but now it was full of love. Previously he had rejected God because of what he blamed God for doing with his father. Now he had asked forgiveness for that resentment and he was reunited with his Father. He put it this way: "I hated God because I blamed Him for Dad's death. I struggled with this hatred for a long time. Finally, by His Spirit, God expressed His love to me and I opened my heart to Him. As soon as I opened my heart, I was a different person and I knew it."

God wants us, too, to ask forgiveness for those things which we had been resentful about. We are creations of God and He knows what is best for us. God wants us to thank Him for the way He made us. Then we can see God's purpose in them.

It wasn't until Lisa thanked God for moving her to

California that she was able to creatively make new friendships. Moses would not have been usable to God if he had not realized that God had given him all the abilities he needed. So, too, we must be thankful to God for what appears to be "weakness" from our viewpoint, recognizing that we are "perfect" from God's point of view.

Betsy is one of the most popular girls I have ever met and I had always thought that she was an attractive girl. One day I was with another guy and he asked, "What is it about Betsy that is so appealing?" I had never really thought about it before. Her hair was curly, her eyes were big and droopy, and her body was nothing to brag about. There was nothing physical that really made her pretty. After much discussion, we decided that it was her spirit and her personality that was so beautiful. She was extremely happy and content with herself. She accepted the person that God made her. Because she had accepted herself, others felt free to accept her as well.

There is a guy on the Wheaton College campus, David, who has cerebral palsy. And yet, this guy is one of the happiest, most radiant people on campus. He had enough self-discipline to play four years of football and intends to go on to grad school. Why? Because he loves himself and has accepted the person God has made.

These two friends, David and Betsy, make me think of a verse in Proverbs, "A glad heart makes a cheerful countenance, but by sorrow of heart the spirit is broken" (Proverbs 15:13).

Now rather than standing in front of the mirror which hangs on the wall, stand in front of the mirror of

God's Word. In this mirror you will see the person whom God made—YOU!!! God wants each of us to love that person. When we love ourselves, we are free to love others. In fact he says that our love for others is based on the love we have for ourselves. "Love your neighbor as yourself." The extent to which we are able to love others is contingent upon the degree to which we love ourselves.

We can try all we want to be successful in our relationships with members of the opposite sex and yet we will fail if we are unsuccessful in our relationship with ourselves. Dating depends on whether or not we have accepted ourselves. Right now (1) Confess to God—your Creator—any area of your life you have been ungrateful for and (2) thank Him specifically for those things. Love yourself as much as God loves you!

4
Those Old Folks at Home

My son keep your father's commandment,
    and forsake not your mother's teaching.
Bind them upon your heart always;
    tie them about your neck.
When you walk, they will lead you;
    when you lie down, they will watch over you;
    and when you awake, they will talk with you.
For the commandment is a lamp and the teaching a light,
    and the reproofs of discipline are the way of life,
to preserve you from the evil woman,
    from the smooth tongue of the adventuress.

Proverbs 6:20–24

Often we can be ashamed to have our friends meet our parents. When my mother was our second-grade room mother I was scared stiff. "How's she going to go over with the kids? What if they think she's weird? She's so strict and conservative, no one will like her, and then they'll think I'm a real three-dollar bill, too." The day of our first field trip I think I tried to fake being sick, but it didn't work. I was trying everything just so I wouldn't have to be there when my mom made her first appearance. I was so nervous I had stomach cramps by the time we got to school. "Oh, no! What if she wants

to hold my hand or what if she kisses me?" As we pulled
up to the schoolyard I slid lower and lower in my seat
so that no one would recognize me. As soon as we
parked I flew out of the car, ran straight to my room,
and tried to mix unnoticeably among the other students. Then finally the moment came. We were all
seated in our places and there was great enthusiasm
and buzzing because we had the day off from our studies.

"Okay, children!" Mrs. Jacobs called for our attention. "I want you to meet our new room mother, Mrs.
Hartley." I was afraid to open my eyes. I gritted my
teeth and looked across the aisle at my "girl friend,"
Susan. I couldn't believe my ears.

"She's pretty," Susan said. Gradually all the red em-
barrassment drained from my cheeks, and that day I
almost enjoyed myself.

Later, when I left grammar school and entered high
school, God had a lot more to teach me about parents
and the position they were to play in my life. While in
high school our views seemed to grow farther and farther apart. Politically, socially, and religiously my father and I could not see eye to eye. Since I was a Christian, I was sure that I only had to obey God and when
what my dad said differed from what I thought God was
saying I would disobey my dad. Very often I would
disobey with the best of intentions.

Now my father was very strict. If I got home five
minutes late I would have some privileges denied. This
particular night I was at a youth Bible study and prayer
meeting. There was a girl there whom I hadn't seen for
a long time and who had been straying from Jesus. The

meeting was a good one and it lasted a few minutes longer than usual. I couldn't go home—I just had to minister to this girl. As it turned out, I talked with her for almost an hour and then, being led by the Spirit, we prayed together. God really met her needs. I then left and ended up pulling in the driveway at ten thirty, half an hour later than I had told my dad I would be home. As I was putting the car away, he met me in the garage with a wrathful expression on his face.

"Where have you been?" he asked.

I arrogantly replied, "I've been about my Father's business." At the time the play on words passed by as being perfectly "spiritual" in my eyes.

I really praise God now that I had such patient parents who were willing to bear with the foolishness of their son. My father would stay up with me night after night into the morning hours talking out my thoughts with me. Looking back now, I must have sounded so foolish, and yet I thought I was a real "spiritual Joe." Even though my ideas sounded heretical and blasphemous to him, Dad hung in there. Through the whole process God took me through, I must say that my dad remained my closest friend. By the senior year of high school my dad and I got along perfectly and we have ever since. The difference was that I learned to be submissive in the relationship.

Parents Are the Number One Responsibility

Joanne was having one of those mountaintop experiences. God's Spirit worked in a mighty way in the lives of about thirty kids one Sunday evening before an evening service. He poured out great conviction and everyone was moved to tears of repentance; there were spontaneous songs and several were given the gift of tongues. Out of that experience, God brought about fifteen teenagers, including Joanne, together in a very closely knit fellowship group. We met twice a week for prayer and Bible study.

One night Joanne arrived all upset. "My parents told me not to come tonight. In fact, they told me that I can't come anymore." She pouted. "So, I decided to come only once a week."

We all rallied around her in prayer. God showed us that even that one night a week was not righteous. God gave us a verse:

> Children, obey your parents in the Lord, for this is right. "Honor your father and mother" (this is the first commandment with a promise), "that it may be well with you and that you may live long on the earth."
>
> Ephesians 6: 1–3

Satan was making things even harder for her by lying to her. He said to her, "Well, that's stupid; your parents aren't even behaving like Christians. Your parents are just too strict. You won't have any fellowship with other Christians. What if you fall away?" The list went on and on. Satan was trying desperately to convince Joanne that Jesus didn't mean what He said.

Although she couldn't answer all her questions, she obeyed by faith. For two weeks I didn't see her. The various members of the fellowship group would pray for her, but they would only see her going to and from classes during school.

God gave Joanne a verse from Proverbs to pray in faith: "The king's heart [or parents] is a stream of water in the hand of the LORD: he turns it wherever he will" (Proverbs 21:1). She knew that it takes time for the course of a stream to change direction, but she believed God. Even though her father opposed much of her "Christian fanaticism," Joanne obeyed God's voice through him. She wanted to go to a Christian college and her father wanted her to go to a secular school, so she left her desires with God; she wanted to pursue a missions career and her father wanted her to pursue a "normal life," so she left her desires with God.

Two weeks had passed and I got a call from one of the brothers in our fellowship, "Fred, how would you like to go Christmas caroling tonight?"

"Sure, that sounds good to me. Where do you want to go?"

"Oh, didn't you hear? Joanne's parents want us to go over there. They're going to give us refreshments too."

When I "regained consciousness" I told him I wouldn't miss it for anything.

We got there and her parents were extremely friendly. Before we went out to sing in the neighborhood, we got in a circle and held hands to pray. We asked God to reveal Jesus to those who didn't know Him, as we sang. This was the killer!

In walked Joanne's dad. Everyone just about choked when he said, "Hey, what are you kids doing?"

"Ah, ah . . . we're praying, would you like to join us?" I apologetically interjected after a few awkward seconds.

He got in the circle and started right in, "Hey, God. I really think this is great to have these kids talkin' with You like this. . . ." We just praised God silently then, but when we got outside, did we ever let loose a "Hallelujah" that must have been heard for miles away.

We later asked Joanne what caused the change with her mom and dad. She told us that for a long time it seemed like a hopeless case. She said it seemed that no matter what she would do for them they wouldn't respond. Regardless, she happily did whatever they asked. When she had finished doing what they asked, she would ask them what else she could do. Joanne even made some extra things for her dad to eat. When they would ask why she was doing so much, she would tell them one of two things: "Because I love you," or "God speaks to me through you and I can please and obey Him by pleasing and obeying you." In that brief period of time God changed Joanne's parents. Within two years they were happy to send her to a Christian college where she would prepare for the mission field. Today her family is a happy one, unified in Christian love.

Joanne learned that her first responsibility was to her parents and that their hearts were certainly in God's hands. By obeying them, even when she didn't feel like it, she even convinced her parents that they were in God's hands. She stayed home every night of the week because she believed God: "Children, obey your parents in everything, for this pleases the Lord" (Colossians 3:20). The Lord Jesus was pleased and He cast a large mountain into the sea. When we stood in the circle asking God to touch lives through our singing, little did we know that one of those lives would be within Joanne's home.

We Must Earn Responsibility, Never Demand it

No matter what the responsibility might be, it is certainly our natural desire to demand it rather than seeking to earn it. Sometimes it's hard to accept that the first responsibility is our parents, but until we have learned to love, honor, and obey them God is not going to give us any other responsibilities. Joanne could have demanded the right to go to church. In fact, she did sneak out without her parents knowing it a few times. But God was not working in her life the way He wanted to at that time. It wasn't until she gave up the right to go out with her friends, whether it be on a date or to a Bible study, that the Spirit of God really went to work in her family and in her own life.

There is a long list of responsibilities that we can demand from our parents.

1. Time: when to get in, what chores to do (or not to do).

2. Friends, reputation: whom to spend your time with.

3. Money: how to spend it.

4. Appearance: what clothes to wear.

5. Possessions: what music you buy and how loud you play it.

Have you ever tried to demand a responsibility?

Have you ever said to yourself, "Aw, I'm old enough to decide what time I'm going to come home. I don't have to listen to them anymore." Or, "They can't tell me what to do with my life or what college to go to." Or, "Just because they want me to mow the lawn this Saturday, I'm going to the football game." Or, "Who are they to tell me not to go to church?" Or perhaps more likely, "Who are they to tell me to go to church?"

Believe me, I know all about struggling for responsibilities. Once, I was on the way out the door on a big date when my dad called me back. "What is that you have on?" he questioned. After he saw it, I was sent back to my room to change. He didn't think that boys should wear pink pants. I changed and was on the way out the door again. "Hey, Fred, where are you going? You're dressed for a rodeo, not for a movie. I think you ought to go back and change again."

Before I was on the way to pick up my date I had changed five or six times. I was not pleased with what my father had me do, but I did it.

The list of responsibilities that God intends for us to earn is a mile long. However, when He thinks we are ready to handle them, He will have our parents give us the responsibility.

Can you imagine being a junior in high school and having to be home at ten o'clock on the weekend? That was what my father insisted on. Now, I thought that was a little harsh, and for longer than a year I fought it quite a bit. I would always come home a few minutes later than that and I would always get in some kind of trouble. Sometimes it was worse than others. But after a while I gave in. "If you can't beat 'em, join 'em." I must admit my social life didn't exactly thrive with a ten o'clock curfew, but at least there was peace under the roof.

Through these and other situations God taught me that as a teenager I was never to demand my responsibilities from my parents. God knew what was best for me and He worked through them.

What and Not Who

The verse that knocked me off my high horse was this one: "The eye that mocks a father and scorns to obey a mother will be picked out by the ravens of the valley and eaten by the vultures" (Proverbs 30:17). So often I would look at my father when he'd crack a corny joke and think, "Oh, you think you're real funny, don't you?" He used to have this sweater that I thought was just horrible. It was a mohair with buttons up the front. It seemed as though he would wear it every day. I'd say to myself, "Man, what's with you? Don't you have any class at all?" When he'd make me come in early I'd have a series of critical thoughts that I would say then, too. My eye was mocking my father. I was guilty. And my mother. . . .

There were certain things that she would have me do that I hated. Every night . . ."Fred, would you take out the garbage?" My list of duties around the house was not very long, but they were always there. Whenever they came up I would resent it terribly. I scorned to obey my mother. I was guilty.

Then I read another verse. "If one curses his father or his mother, his lamp will be put out in utter darkness" (Proverbs 20:20). Oh, no! Proverbs was ripping me to shreds.

With these verses in mind I knew that I had to have some sort of change. I didn't know exactly what to do, but I felt too guilty to brush it aside. For two weeks or so I did everything they asked me to do and even a little extra to help my guilt feelings. It really didn't help very much.

I read further and there it was. "Children, obey your parents in the Lord, for this is right. *'Honor* your father and mother' (this is the first commandment with a promise), "that it may be well with you and that you may live long on the earth' " (Ephesians 6:1–3). That promise was quite different from "my eye being picked by the ravens and eaten by the vultures." The word that I didn't know anything about was *honor*. I had learned to obey. I wore the style of clothes that my parents liked. I came in at ten o'clock. I took out the garbage, and so forth. But honor? That was something different.

In the next years God was going to teach me a lot about honor that I would never forget.

It doesn't matter *who* our parents are. The only thing that matters is *what* they are! Parents have a unique authority in children's lives, not because they have a good sense of humor, because they dress sharp, or because they are spiritual. The only thing that gives parents authority is the mere fact that they are parents. Joanne learned that God wanted to use her parents to teach her patience. By her honoring their position in her life she could be confident of knowing God's will.

I had previously thought that because my parents were so out of it, I didn't have to listen to them. What they are like does not matter. What they *are* is all that matters.

Obedience is outward, but honor is inward. Obedience is an action of the will, but honor is of the spirit. Honor is not shown to a person, it is shown to a position. Because a person has a position of authority, he or she is to be honored.

Mom and Dad: God's Hand

> Likewise you that are younger [children] be subject to the elders [parents]. Clothe yourselves, all of you, with humility toward one another, for "God opposes the proud but gives grace to the humble."
>
> Humble yourselves therefore under the mighty hand of God, that in due time he may exalt you. Cast all your anxieties on him for he cares about you.
>
> 1 Peter 5:5–7

I learned that God spoke to me through my parents. When my parents asked me to get in at a certain hour, God was asking me to get in at a certain hour. If they asked me to pass the mashed potatoes, God was asking me to pass the mashed potatoes. Every one of their words was God's word to me. Jesus said, "If you love Me, you will keep My commandments." It was a joy to my heart to obey my parents and to honor them, because I was loving Jesus as I was loving them. When I would submit to my parents' hand of authority, I was really submitting to God's hand of authority.

When I was in high school, there was a phrase that my mother would keep repeating that I just couldn't stand. She called it "the absolute yes" or "the absolute no." It would go something like this.

The phone would ring. I would answer, "Hello. Oh, hi, Jeff. Well, just a minute and let me ask. Hey, Mom, can I go play tennis?"

"No."

"Aw, come on, Mom, just for a little while?"

"Fred, you've heard 'the absolute no'! "

"Jeff, there's no way. She said no! Bye."

That was it. There was no budging the absolute no or yes. This is the way parents should be regarded—as the final word.

You might be saying to yourself, "What a drag! This kid never got to do anything on his own. He was nothin' but a robot." These thoughts are certainly natural, but they clearly miss the point.

When Joanne submitted to her parents and decided not to go to church or go out on dates until her parents said she could, what happened? *God exalted her!* This is the purpose of submission—so that God will lift us up —this is earning responsibility.

When I submitted to my parents in everything, do you know what happened? By my senior year I could make practically every decision I wanted to and there was perfect trust and peace between my parents and me. Through submission, I had earned responsibility.

It's Not Easy

Is obedience of this sort easy? No. Not at all. That's why God tells us, "Cast all your anxieties on Him, for He cares for you."

Art and George are two brothers who are both Christians. Their father is very strict and extremely demanding of their time. There are hardly enough hours in the day to get all the work done that their father gives them to do. They work for twelve to sixteen hours a day. Art is very submissive and willingly does whatever his dad requests, and because of this his parents will listen to what he has to say. George, on the other hand, is quite different. He will sit around telling his father all about Jesus, how he needs to be born again, and that he is a sinner going to hell.

For a while God was dealing with the father. But George never did any work around the house. He was always out to Bible studies and so forth. Their father was hungry for love, and yet these two brothers were working against one another. What God intended to do in their father's life was stunted because of the lack of obedience on George's part.

Was it any easier for Art than for his brother to obey their strict father? Not at all. The only difference was that Art believed God and relied on Him, while George relied on his own understanding and copped out on his responsibilities to God as well as to his father.

About once every month Art would come up to me after church or give me a call during the day to ask for prayer. "Hey, Fred, things are getting pretty tough around here. Will you pray for me?" Art went on to tell me about how his father would slug him and scream curses at him whenever he used a word like "Bible," "church," or "Jesus."

"Art, I really praise God for you. You are right where God wants you and you're submitting." Before we would hang up we would cast all the anxieties on God. Art grew a lot through those difficult times. This is what it means: "God opposes the proud but gives grace to the humble." When Art realized that his father's words were his Father's words obedience came a lot easier.

For a while Art really struggled with this physical and verbal abuse. In no way did it come naturally for him to refrain from answering back. But after six months he is seeing some results. I received a letter from Art recently in which he told me how his father told him that he loved him, something that he had never said before. In fact, his father asked Art's advice on some things. Art went on to say, "God couldn't have done anything better for me than to let me suffer under my father. Fred, I have just grown so much through this! Praise Jesus!"

Satan or Submission

After I graduated from college a friend told me he had a very serious drug problem and that he was sleeping with a girl every night. He asked me to pray for his deliverance from this wickedness. As I looked at him I prayed silently, and the Spirit had me ask, "Are you living with your parents?"

"No. Why do you ask?" He was stunned by the question.

"Well, I'm not surprised. You see, you have no protection from the enemy of our souls because you're out of submission. You're a sitting duck for Satan." I continued, "To answer your question, no, I won't pray for your deliverance."

He was flabbergasted.

I went on to share a few verses with him.

> Be sober, be watchful. Your adversary the devil prowls around like a roaring lion, seeking some one to devour. Resist him, firm in your faith, knowing that the same experience of suffering is required of your brotherhood throughout the world.
>
> 1 Peter 5:8, 9

I told him how a roaring lion is not a harmful one. "A lion who roars is an old lion without any teeth who seeks to scare its game out of the protected area into the grasp of younger lions waiting silently elsewhere. This is how Satan seeks to attack Christian youths. We are to be under submission to our parents. The roaring lion will come up to us and scream, 'Aw, those parents of yours are too strict!' or 'They can't tell you to do that!' These are nothing but harmless accusations. The devil never arrives at the truth. Our instructions are very clear; 'stand firm in your faith.' This clearly means to obey, stay in submission and follow their instructions. In fact whenever Satan tells you not to obey, be extra sure to obey."

I continued, "There is another verse in Proverbs that

says 'He is a shield to those who walk in integrity' (Proverbs 2:7). When you are not walking in submission, you are not walking in integrity. Therefore God can't shield you from Satan's attack."

He looked back at me as if I had told him everything he had ever done. When I felt he was ready for more I asked him, "Have your parents ever warned you about sexual immorality?" I really didn't have to ask but I wanted him to understand what I was saying.

"Yeah." After a pause, he said, "I see what you mean."

"Now I have one more question for you. Will you go back and live with your parents?" He sat there in silence. After a while he had an embarrassed laugh and said, "Boy, I really don't think I could say for sure."

Unfortunately he was not willing to make the vow that God wanted him to. I begged him not to leave my room until he purposed in his heart to submit to and honor his parents. But he left the same way that he entered my room. He has been defeated and harassed ever since. He has been strangled by moral guilt and loose sexual relations as have so many others who are just like him. He knew that his parents would not approve of the girl he had been dating and that his lifestyle would have to change drastically.

Before he left my room I read to him from Proverbs:

> My son, keep your father's commandment,
>   And forsake not your mother's teaching.
> Bind them upon your heart always;
>   tie them about your neck.

When you walk, they will lead you;
> when you lie down, they will watch over you;
> and when you awake, they will talk with you.
For the commandment is a lamp and the teaching a light,
> and the reproofs of discipline are the way of life,
to preserve you from the evil woman,
> from the smooth tongue of the adventuress.

Proverbs 6:20–24

God intends to give us spiritual protection as we submit to our parents, but we make ourselves sitting ducks for Satan when we rebel and set ourselves up as our own independent authorities. We must not forget that Satan was the first one to rebel against God's authority. When we rebel we are sons of rebellion. As it says: "Let no one deceive you in any way; for that day will not come, unless the rebellion comes first, and the man of lawlessness is revealed, the son of perdition, who opposes and exalts himself against every so-called god or object of worship . . . for the mystery of lawlessness is already at work . . ." (2 Thessalonians 2:3, 4, 7). A few of the characteristics of people in these last days are, " . . . lovers of self, lovers of money, proud, arrogant, abusive, disobedient to their parents, ungrateful . . ." (2 Timothy 3:2).

What About Me?

Ask yourself, "What about me?" "Am I honoring my mom? Do I seek for God to speak to me through my father? Am I in submission to my parents? Or is Satan getting the victory in my life?" Do you get embarrassed when other people meet your parents? Do you listen to what your parents say as the final word?

God has something He wants you to tell Him: "Father, thanks for Mom and Dad. I know that You gave them to me for a special purpose. Right now, I submit to them and will listen to what You have to tell me through them. They are more important than ———, ———, ———, (list the specific things you have previously demanded). I lay all these on Your altar. I know that their hearts are in Your hands. I praise You for the protection You give me through them and for the direction You will give my life through them. As I submit to them I know that I am submitting to You. Hallelujah!"

Coming under submission very often includes obtaining forgiveness for pride and lack of love in our pasts. If so, you will be amazed at how much more your parents know about your past than you think they know.

So what does all this have to do with dating? Primarily, "that special someone" is never to gain greater importance in an unmarried life than one's parents. God never intended a teenager to be out every night of the week with a certain guy or girl. Home life is a higher priority than dating life.

Also, as we have seen, parents do have a say as to whom we should and should not go out with. In fact, they have the final say. We should certainly remember the words of Solomon, "To preserve you from the evil woman. . . ." I was always amazed at how much my mother could tell about a girl just by meeting her one time.

One of the greatest things a guy or girl can do before going out on a date is to request prayer from their mother or father. I know from experience and from observation that a boy-girl relationship is one of the easiest areas of a young life in which to get out from under the submission of God. Because of the excitement and "romance" it can very easily possess our thoughts day and night. This is unrighteous. One of the best ways to avoid this is to always maintain a higher priority in your relationship with your parents and to seek counsel from them. Dating is not a time to leave "those old folks at home."

5
He Loves Me; He Lusts Me Not

For freedom Christ has set us free; stand fast therefore, and do not submit again to a yoke of slavery.
. . . And those who belong to Christ Jesus have crucified the flesh with its passions and desires.

Galatians 5:1, 24

Pierre was a foreign exchange student from France.
He was loud, aggressive, and influential in the high
school. He was very athletic—excelling in soccer—and
a leader among the students. He was always setting
trends in clothing, styles, and life-styles. Unfortunately,
as I look back on his high school, he had a very negative
influence.

Pierre made it his goal to go to bed with every girl
he went out with. He was several years ahead of me
in school, so I did not know him personally, but his
conquests were in everyone's conversations. He had
a genuine following of distant admirers. That was
one thing that always confused me—everyone stood
at a distance from him. I would say that he was the
most liked and yet the most hated person in the
school.

There were several inconsistencies in his life that
were apparent to all who knew him, even from a dis-

tance. He had a horrible temper, and although he would always try to come across with this carefree attitude, he was often angry and deeply frustrated. It seemed that he was never satisfied and would always have to get into some greater sexual perversion. He was constantly getting in arguments with teachers, coaches, and friends. After he was in the school for a few months he was friendless, bored, and empty.

When Pierre first got to school he would tell everyone, "Man, I'm free. I'm free. What's wrong with you?" He even convinced a few to follow his hedonistic lifestyle. However, within a few months he learned that the freedom he proclaimed was really bondage.

I am reminded of these verses: "With their high-sounding nonsense they use the sensual pull of the lower passions to attract those who were just on the point of cutting loose from their companions in evil. They promise them liberty. Liberty!—when they themselves are bound hand and foot to utter depravity" (2 Peter 2: 18, 19 PHILLIPS).

Every person who has ever taken a stand for Jesus Christ has been hit in the face with fleshly temptations. There are "Pierres" in every school. If they are not in the form of a single person they can be represented by the popular opinion. How often it is said, "Well, everyone else does it, so why shouldn't I?"

As I mentioned in the first chapter of this book, if you wanted to read popular opinion you've got the wrong man. I'm not going to give it to you. God's way has never been popular. If you want to be a disciple of Jesus Christ, you don't look at the way the world does things. If you want your dating life to be in submission to the

Lord Jesus Christ don't give me that "Well, nobody lives that way any more" line.

When the question comes up, "As a Christian, how far can I go on a date?" so many will respond, "The Bible doesn't give us any guidelines." This is an unfortunate lie. The Bible gives very clear answers to this question, but we must realize that God's thoughts are not our thoughts and His ways are not our ways. The reason why few people take a stand on the issue is because Jesus' standards are very strict. There is no doubt about that.

Speaking as a boy who had to deal with healthy sexual drives, the following sex perspective should be helpful in your life, as it was in mine.

Lust, Not Legalism

In the Old Testament God gave the people specific laws about what they could and could not do with regards to sex. (Read it for yourself if you would like in Leviticus 18–20.) In the New Testament God changes His vocabulary and tightens His demands. Jesus shows this distinction when He says, "You have heard that it was said, 'You shall not commit adultery.' But I say to you that every one who looks at a woman lustfully has already committed adultery with her in his heart" (Matthew 5: 27, 28).

For us then, the gauge for what is right and what is wrong is the gauge of lust. Lustful desires give way to sin whenever they are dwelt upon or appealed to (*see* James 1:14, 15).

If you have ever read Mark, Romans, 2 Corinthians,

Galatians, Ephesians, Colossians, 1 Thessalonians, Jude, or James you have come across the following words and you probably have not known what they mean. *Lasciviousness* is the tendency towards lustful desires. *Sensuality* is a planned appeal towards sexual desires (like, "Hey, do you want to go to the drive-in?"). *Concupiscence* is a strong abnormal appetite for sexual involvement. Thus, the words which God uses to point out the right and wrong of sexual relations are words describing different levels of lust. Lust is the gauge. Even lasciviousness, which is simply "the tendency towards lustful desires," is sinful. In fact in Galatians 5:19–21 God tells us that the person who is lascivious will not get into heaven.

Pure Hearts See God

A while ago I went to see Brenda, whom I hadn't seen for a long time. I had previously had good fellowship with her but she was no longer attending our Bible studies and I wondered why. I had heard rumors, but I wanted to go to her personally and get the facts straight.

Brenda's car was in the driveway as I pulled up so I quickly prayed, "Lord Jesus, give me wisdom and discernment. Show me right where she's at and how to minister to her." She answered the door and we sat in the den and talked. "I haven't seen you for a while and I was wondering how you're doing."

"Oh . . . I guess I'm all right."

After a bit more surface talk I asked, "Where are your thoughts about Jesus these days?"

She blushed, even though she knew that it was coming. "Well, I guess you could say that I really don't believe in Him anymore."

"Hm." I paused and thought.

"Are you dating anyone, Brenda?"

"Yes."

"Do I know him?"

"No."

"Is he a Christian?"

"No."

"Have you known each other very long?"

"No."

"Do you know each other very well?" I expected her to answer *yes* and she did.

"I hope this is not too personal, and if you don't want to answer you don't have to, but are you physically involved with one another?"

I realized she felt as though she was backed right into a corner. She was quite embarrassed and apologetically answered, "Yes, how did you know?"

She was right; I did know. From the first statement she made about not believing in Jesus anymore I could tell that there was most likely a moral problem.

To answer her question I asked her to get a Bible and I showed her two verses. First I read her, "Blessed are the pure in heart, for they shall see God."

"You see, everyone is born with a capacity to know God and to believe in Him. Have you ever noticed how little children accept whatever they are told about God?"

"Yeah. My little cousin is a real religious fanatic."

"Well, you might think she is a fanatic, but you used

to be a lot more zealous than she is." Brenda was rather taken back by that one. She did remember and was sorry for those memories.

"The reason children believe in God is because they have pure hearts." Then I turned to Psalm 14 and read, "The fool says in his heart, 'There is no God.' They are corrupt, they do abominable deeds, there is none that does good" (Psalms 14:1, 2).

I continued to explain to her, "The opposite of a pure heart is a dirty heart—one which is 'corrupt' and does 'abominable deeds.' What does this man say?" I handed her the Bible and had her read it herself.

Very quietly and slowly she read, "There is no God," and handed the Bible back to me.

"Before you became physically involved did you question whether it was right or wrong?"

"Yes. I sure did," she said slowly and thoughtfully.

"When you first began to have sexual relations in even the smallest ways, did you have any guilt feelings?"

At this point she couldn't look me in the face but she said, "Yes. I was guilty."

I took the Bible and turned to 1 Timothy and read:

Cling tightly to your faith in Christ and always keep your conscience clear, doing what you know is right. For some people have disobeyed their consciences and have deliberately done what they knew was wrong. It isn't surprising that soon they lost their faith in Christ after defying God like that.

1 Timothy 1:19 LB

I continued questioning, "When you felt guilty and your conscience was saying *no*, did you disobey your conscience?" She didn't respond because the question was rhetorical. She realized she had rejected her conscience. As we briefly sat in silence I breathed a prayer, "Oh, Lord, move her to repentance."

"But I don't believe anymore!" she blurted out. "You are too late. I think that all this Jesus stuff is a bunch of lies. If it does you some good that's just fine but don't force it on anybody else. My boyfriend is a great guy. He really cares about me. We have a good time and I don't see anything wrong with anything we're doing." She spoke very nervously, almost violently.

Maybe it was too late, I thought. She was a lot more resentful than I expected her to be. But I prayed, "Oh, Lord, move her to repentance."

After we just kind of sat there looking around the room saying nothing, I looked over at her and I could tell the Spirit was working in her heart. "Do you think God still loves me?" she asked.

"Yup."

She looked at the floor as if she really wasn't convinced.

"Do you think that after several thousand years of sin and wickedness, all of a sudden a few things that you do wrong are going to change the nature of God?"

She smiled.

"You know what God wants you to do?" I asked as I flipped through the Bible and read her a few verses. . . .

"God's plan is to make you holy, and that means a

clean cut with sexual immorality" (1 Thessalonians 4:3 PHILLIPS).

I paused and asked her, "If you follow the advice of these verses, what is it going to do to your relationship with this boy?"

She was impressed at how right-on the truth of Scripture was as the Spirit of God applied it to her life. "Well, I guess it would cut it off."

I nodded in agreement and read on, "Every one of you should learn to control his body, keeping it pure and treating it with respect, and never allowing it to fall victim to lust, as do the pagans with no knowledge of God" (1 Thessalonians 4:4, 5 PHILLIPS).

It was obvious that the reason she wondered whether God still loved her or not was because she really didn't love herself. She wasn't treating herself with respect.

I read on, "You cannot break this rule without cheating your fellow-men. Indeed God will punish all who do offend in this matter, as we have plainly told you and warned you. The calling of God is not to impurity but to the most thorough purity, and anyone who makes light of the matter is not making light of a man's ruling but of God's command. It is not for nothing that the Spirit God gives us is called the *Holy* Spirit" (1 Thessalonians 4: 6–9 PHILLIPS).

"Do you feel that God is calling you to purity, Brenda?"

Very seriously she replied, "Yes, I think so."

"Well, as I have just read, 'that entails first of all a clean cut with sexual immorality.' You haven't forgotten how to pray, have you?" She looked over at me and smiled.

I felt that I had done all God sent me there for, so I left. As I sat in the car before I turned on the ignition, I bowed my head, "Lord Jesus, I praise You for speaking to her and for showing Your love to her. Right now make her obedient to the words You spoke to her. Thanks."

Brenda, like so many others, was a devout follower of the Lord Jesus, but she was enticed, deceived, and held slave by her lustful desires. That pure heart that used to see God had been clouded over with sin and guilt. Very subtly she rationalized away her guilt and arrived at her own moral code, concluding that the Bible was a fantasy. She lost respect for herself because of her sinfulness and lost sight of God's love for her. But as we talked she did one thing right. She was honest before God. She admitted her guilt feelings and gave an open ear to the God she used to believe in.

Not only had Brenda's belief in God changed, but many other characteristics of her personality changed. She had previously been a very creative girl and done very well in school. During this period, her grades dropped way off and she was very withdrawn. Her parents complained of how her other relationships dropped off and how irritable and very argumentative she was around the house.

The reason for this change in Brenda's behavior is that sin affects the soul. We read ". . . abstain from the passions of the flesh that wage war against your soul" (1 Peter 2:11). The soul sees God. The soul is creative. The soul is responsible for a person's character. When Brenda sinned she sinned against her soul, and all areas of her life were affected. Her freedom became bondage, her peace became frustration, her creativity became boredom, and her happiness became guilt and emptiness. As it says in Proverbs 14:30, "A tranquil mind gives life to the flesh, but passion makes the bones rot."

Who said God doesn't have anything to say about how far we can go on dates? God intends our friendships to be creative and fulfilling. Therefore, He sets down very definite moral standards.

Anything which causes lust and appeals to our own fleshly desires is sinful as well as harmful. I have yet to meet anyone who can engage in even the slightest form of petting without arousing passions. Petting, therefore, is certainly sinful. This also would certainly indicate that certain forms of kissing would be wrong—even more minor forms of touching.

God intends for our whole lives to be Spirit-led and Spirit-filled. Our dating lives are no exception. There are many teenagers who regard themselves as Spirit-filled Christians, who even read the Bible three hours a day or speak in tongues and yet give themselves over to every form of fleshly sex sin imaginable.

We are exhorted in Galatians 5:16, 17, "But I say, walk by the Spirit, and do not gratify the desires of the flesh. For the desires of the flesh are against the Spirit, and the desires of the Spirit are against the flesh; for these are opposed to each other, to prevent you from doing what you would." To pray for the leading of the Spirit of God in your life and then to engage in some sort of lustful activity is declaring war on your soul. The two are opposites and this is mockery to God.

The first three works of the flesh listed in the next

verses in Galatians 5 are all sex sins: "fornication, impurity, licentiousness." Remember that licentiousness is only the "tendency toward lustful desires." The rest of the works of the flesh follow the sex sins. Once any sexual immorality has been committed, strife, jealousy, selfishness, and a partying spirit are sure to follow. It is amazing to watch boy-girl relationships fall apart when lust enters in. As soon as sex is resorted to, things begin to decay. Arguments, insecurity over the true affections of the other person, lack of real concern for the other person, and a more self-centered interest all follow.

Even regarding a tendency toward lustful desires, Paul says, "I warn you as I warned you before, that those who do such things shall not inherit the Kingdom of God" (Galatians 5:21b). This needs no further comment.

In stark contrast to the fruits of a lustful relationship is the fruit of a Spirit-led relationship ". . . love, joy, peace, patience, kindness, goodness, faithfulness, gentleness, self-control."

Let's line the fruit up against one another:

Fruit of Lust	Fruit of the Spirit
Selfishness	Love
Boredom	Joy
Anger	Peace
Aggressiveness	Patience
Strife	Kindness
Envy	Goodness
Jealousy	Faithfulness
Enmity	Gentleness
Party-spirit	Self-control

How true these words are in a dating relationship: ". . . whatever a man sows, that will he also reap. For he who sows to his own flesh will from the flesh reap corruption; but he who sows to the Spirit will from the Spirit reap eternal life" (Galatians 6:7, 8). I think that everyone in the world would prefer the fruit of love to the works of lust. And yet, very few are willing to sow in the Spirit.

The Price of Freedom

The church at Corinth was somewhat like a lot of churches and fellowship groups are today. They were really strong Christians in their own eyes, a lot of prophecies, speaking in tongues, and miracles; but sex sin was rampant. They were taking the freedom they received from Christ and using it as a license for all manner of wickedness. In response to this abused freedom Paul wrote, " 'All things are lawful for me,' but not all things are helpful. 'All things are lawful for me,' but I will not be enslaved by anything" (1 Corinthians 6:12).

Mark and I were walking along, and he was talking about a girl he was dating. Discerning that there was some immorality in his life I asked, "What's your view of sex before marriage?"

He smiled just as if I caught him with his hand in a cookie jar. "Why do you ask?"

"Oh, well, if you don't want to answer it's okay. It was a rather personal question, I'll admit."

"No. I don't mind telling you. I have nothing to hide.

I think it depends. In certain cases I think it's okay."

"What does the Bible have to say?" I knew that he had gone to more Bible studies than I had and I really expected him to know.

He looked back at me with a sadly embarrassed expression. "I don't know." His answer surprised me.

"Would you mind if I showed you?"

"No." He replied apprehensively.

So I proceeded. I took him through different Scriptures and I could tell I wasn't getting anywhere. I stopped and waited for him to respond.

"Yeah. I've heard all that before, but God forgives me of anything I do wrong and besides, I'm free from the Law."

"Mark, you're free from the Law. But, tell me, are you free?"

"Hey, what do you mean? Free from what?"

"Are you just plain old 'free'?"

"I don't understand. What do you mean 'free'?"

"Well, Mark, what do *you* mean 'free'?"

Now he was getting a little upset. He knew that there was something that I knew that he didn't and he was getting rather hot. At the time he didn't know that I was loving him. "I mean I'm free. I can do whatever I want to. I can go wherever I want with whomever I please."

The "I . . . I . . . I . . ." was showing through. "Mark, if you are really free, don't go out with her tonight. I don't think God wants you to." I read to him from Second Peter 2: "Their eyes cannot look at a woman without lust and they miss no opportunity for sin. They captivate the unstable ones, and their technique of getting what they want is, through long practice, highly developed" (2 Peter 2:14 PHILLIPS).

"Mark, you're not free. You have to go out. You have to satisfy your desires." I read him: *All things are lawful for me, but I will not be enslaved by anything.* "Are you really free?"

"Well . . ." he thought deeply. "I get what you mean."

"You see, Mark, what happens is when we disobey God we become slaves to disobedience. When we obey God we are slaves of righteousness and of God. The best definition of freedom I have ever heard is this: 'Freedom is not the license to do what you want; it's the power to do what you ought.' "

God intends for all of our boy-girl relationships to be in freedom. "For freedom Christ has set us free; stand fast therefore and do not submit again to a yoke of slavery." Lust and passion are real chains of bondage which truly destroy the freedom Christ won for us on the cross.

Mark was bound hand and foot by the pull of his lower nature and to my knowledge he never repented, nor was he delivered from sexual immorality. He, as so many others like him, was not willing to submit to God's limitations in his dating life.

Jesus came to pronounce release to the captive and he desires to set each of us free.

I have seen many, many teenagers (including myself) regain the freedom Christ provided for us. There is a price involved; the price of saying *no* to our desires and saying *yes* to God's limitations. Self-control is a fruit produced in each of us when we yield the right-of-way to the Spirit of God. Many who were bound hand and foot to the driving sensual desires of the flesh have gained total freedom in their dating relationships. The following two chapters are dedicated to how to receive such deliverance as well as how to maintain the freedom of the Holy Spirit in a boy-girl relationship.

6
Regaining Freedom

God's plan is to make you holy, and that means a
clean cut with sexual immorality.

1 Thessalonians 4:3 PHILLIPS

Kim had been a Christian for a year or so, but she was
not walking in fellowship with Jesus. There were thorns
in her life crowding out the good seed, as Jesus depicts
in the parable of the sower. (*See* Mark 4.) She was very
popular and the thrills of good times seemed more appealing to her than following Jesus.

On a Thursday night Sherry called her and asked her
to come to our youth meeting. She very reluctantly said
yes because this had been the third time Sherry called
her and she didn't have the heart to say *no* again. She
came and the Spirit of God really spoke to her heart. It
was a glorious reunion between her and her Lord.

Not very long after this Calvin began to ask her out.
She thought it was fantastic because she never had a
Christian boyfriend before. On the second or third date
he began to get "hot and heavy" . . . he really tried to
put the moves on her. There was talk of marriage and
many other inappropriate details. She was scared and
came to me for some advice.

We went right to the Word for instruction. First I

turned to Second Timothy and had her read it: "All scripture is inspired by God and profitable for teaching, for reproof, for correction, and for training in righteousness . . ." (2 Timothy 3:16).

I interrupted her. "For training in what?"

"Righteousness," she said with a smile. " . . . That the man [or woman] of God may be complete, equipped for every good work" (2 Timothy 3:17).

I went on to take her on a little tour through the Word of God to see what it had to say about living free from sensuous drives.

The Number One Problem: Parents

"How do you get along with your parents?" was the first question I asked her.

"Oh, we get along fine," she answered very quickly.

My immediate response was to believe her, but I caught myself and asked, "Do you spend much time with them?"

"Oh, no. I'm hardly ever home."

"Hmm? Do they ever give you any advice . . . particularly dating advice?" I further asked.

"Oh, no. They never tell me what to do. They let me do just about whatever I want."

At this point I noticed something that would be difficult to deal with. I read her two different sections of Scripture: Proverbs 6:20–24 and 1 Peter 5:5–9.

My son [or daughter], keep your father's commandment,
    and forsake not your mother's teaching.
Bind them upon your heart always;

tie them about your neck.
When you walk, they will lead you;
  when you lie down, they will watch over you;
  and when you awake, they will talk with you.
For the commandment is a lamp and the teaching a light,
  and the reproofs of discipline are the way of life,
To preserve you from the evil woman [or man], from the
  smooth tongue of the adventuress.

Proverbs 6:20–24

"Advice from parents gives us protection from the temptations of the devil. It says much the same thing in First Peter:

Likewise you that are younger [children] be subject to the elders [parents]. Clothe yourselves, all of you, with humility toward one another, for "God opposes the proud, but gives grace to the humble."

Humble yourselves therefore under the mighty hand of God, that in due time he may exalt you. Cast all your anxieties on him, for he cares about you. Be sober, be watchful. Your adversary the devil prowls around like a roaring lion, seeking some one to devour. Resist him, firm in your faith, knowing that the same experience of suffering is required of your brotherhood throughout the world.

1 Peter 5:5–9

"The way it happens is when we are not under submission to our parents, we are sitting ducks for Satan. He is prowling around seeking to cause children not to submit to their parents.

"Now with you, Kim, your parents don't give you much advice, so you'll have to ask for it. And most importantly, spend a few nights every week home with them. Don't be out with your friends every night of the week even if they are Christian activities. You need the protection of your parents." She wasn't saying anything because she was struck in her heart and there wasn't any need to respond. "Are you ready for any more?" I asked.

"Oh, yeah, this is great!" Kim was a very eager learner. She was after the truth . . . even if it did hurt a little bit.

The Clean Cut

"God tells us that he wants us holy. And the Bible says 'that entails first of all a clean cut with sexual immorality.' What is this going to do with your relationship with Calvin?"

"I guess it's the end."

"Yup."

"But how am I going to do it? What am I going to tell him? He's going to be so upset. I know he won't understand."

"Kim, when you came to me for advice, we decided that we would go to God's Word for our advice, didn't we?"

"Yeah."

"Well, then lets trust His judgment. Okay? Let's just assume that God knows what He's talking about when

He asks us to cut ourselves off from all sexual immorality."

"Okay. I'll do it because I know it is what God wants me to do. But, what do I say to him? I know he's going to call tonight."

"You can start with the truth."

She laughed. "Yeah. Of course. I'll just tell him that God doesn't want us to have that kind of a relationship . . . but we can still go out with each other."

She understood partially, but not completely. I thought it would probably hit hard, but I had to say it sooner or later so I told her. "Kim, I don't think God wants you to date anyone for quite a while." After some awkward silence I explained, "You need to give yourself some time to understand what the real dangers of dating can be and what the purpose of dating is in a Christian's life. You aren't going to work these things out in a night or two."

The next morning Kim called Sherry and was so excited. "I did it. I never thought that I could do it, but I did it. I'm so happy. I can't believe it. Oh! This is so wonderful."

After the air cleared, Sherry asked, "Kim, this sounds great, but what are you talking about?"

"I did it! I told Calvin that God didn't want me to date him anymore and that our relationship was totally fleshly. Boy, I can really see what a mess that would have been. And I'm so glad that I'm free from it now. Praise Jesus! Hallelujah!"

Clear Conscience

The week after, I saw Kim and she looked rather down about something. I waited for her to tell me what it was and she finally said, "I'm down about something, and I really don't know what it is."

Right then God gave to me a word of wisdom and said, "Clear conscience," and I immediately understood everything that she felt. "Would you mind if I showed you some verses in the Word, Kim?"

"No. What do you think I came to you for?"

"That's what I like about you, Kim, you don't mess around. You only want His best. So let's take a look at Matthew 5:

> So if you are offering your gift at the altar, and there remember that your brother has something against you, leave your gift there before the altar and go; first be reconciled to your brother, and then come and offer your gift. Make friends quickly with your accuser, while you are going with him to court, lest your accuser hand you over to the judge, and the judge to the guard, and you be put in prison; truly, I say to you, you will never get out till you have paid the last penny.
>
> Mathew 5:23–26
> Also see Proverbs 6:1–5

As soon as she was done reading the passage I asked, "Do you have anyone in your past that you have a debt with? Is there anyone you have not acted righteously with? Is there a barrier between you and someone else?"

She thought and hesitantly said, "Yes."

"Well, you're not the only one. I've had to ask forgiveness from several people myself. As Jesus says here, we need to go to our accusers and pay our debts or ask forgiveness from them. Until we do ask forgiveness we are held captive by the spirit of wickedness that lead us into sin. Satan has gained that much ground. And he can hold us captive until the debt is removed."

"What do I have to do?" she asked.

"Call up the people you know you have sinned against and ask, 'Will you forgive me for————?' Just fill in the blank with whatever your sin was."

I explained things in greater detail and then Kim started in: "All that sounds impossible. They'll never understand. They'll think that I've really flipped my lid. God's forgiven me. Why should I ask their forgiveness? They probably have forgotten about it already anyway. . . ." On and on she went for about five minutes with very lengthy excuses. When she calmed down, she noticed I was calmly sitting there smiling. She stated, as if there was no use, "Yeah, I know . . . let's just trust His judgment and assume that He knows what He's talking about, right?"

"Yup!" And we went our separate ways.

A couple of weeks later, I saw her again and was very anxious for her to tell me whether she made the phone calls or not. I waited as long as I could for her to tell me about it, until I finally asked her, "Oh, Kim, by the way . . . did you ever make those phone calls and ask forgiveness?"

"Oh, yeah. It wasn't the easiest thing I've ever done but once I started to do it, it was fantastic!"

Kim was gaining a freedom she never knew before.

When I was in high school, I had to make many phone calls—to the tune of forty or more—to girls who I had offended by being insensitive. It is amazing how God wants us to ask forgiveness. I didn't have the phone number of one girl so I called another person to get it. The girl I was trying to reach "just happened to be there." Others said, "This is amazing, I just had a dream about you last night, and I haven't seen you for eight years." Calling a person we haven't seen for a number of years and asking forgiveness for something they might have forgotten is certainly not the easiest thing to do, but it may well be the most valuable. When we ask the Spirit of God to show us who to go to He will not mislead us, and when He pours conviction upon our hearts, we had better be obedient.

There was one phone call that was necessary for me to make that was probably harder than all the others put together. It was one that I had shoved out of my conscious mind. But the Spirit of God dug it up and said, "Make the phone call, *now.*" I hesitated until the pain in my heart was so bad that I could take it no longer. The devil was giving me every reason in the world why I shouldn't call. But I knew that "For the desires of the flesh are against the Spirit, and the desires of the Spirit are against the flesh; for these are opposed to each other to prevent you from doing what you would" (Galatians 5:17). Three times I had the full number dialed and hung up before it rang. Once it even rang and I hung up. The pain of conviction was getting worse and worse, but Satan just did not want to give up that ground. Well, of course God won and I asked forgiveness. But as I was mouthing the words of repentance and then, "Will you forgive me for my lack of love towards you?" I felt as though someone was stabbing me with a long sword through my heart. When the person said, "Why, yes, I forgive you." I felt like the devil himself dropped from my shoulders. Such release and freedom! I was thoroughly exhausted. Jesus won out but the devil fought Him every inch of the way.

That night I slept very deeply, but in the early morning hours I woke up several times and every time I noticed that I was praying in my sleep. Never before had I had this experience. The Spirit of God was free to pray through me even while I was asleep because I was a cleansed vessel.

Just as the Spirit of God deeply convicted me of this ground in my life that Satan had gained, so He desires to convict you of sins that you have not received forgiveness from other people for. Just as Jesus regained this ground in my heart, He desires to regain ground in your life. The Spirit of God should not be hindered in us by debts that we owe other people. Just as Jesus said, "Make friends quickly with your accuser, while you are going with him to court, lest your accuser hand you over to the judge, and the judge to the guard, and you be put in prison; truly, I say to you, you will never get out till you have paid the last penny" (Mathew 5:25, 26). Some offenses are certainly smaller than others. In fact, some may even seem too trivial to consider. Yet a debt is a debt whether one cent or one thousand dollars.

While vacationing in the Florida Keys, I spent one

day snorkeling off a reef in the Gulf. I dove down, saw a large lobster, and speared it. As I swam towards the surface with it dangling from the spear, my friend waved frantically to me. I thought a shark was following me or something. He took his mouthpiece out and said, "Get rid of it! That was illegal."

I didn't know differently so I ripped the tail off and stuffed it in my swim suit. I later learned that ripping the head off is a $3,000 fine. Some time after this I called the Chamber of Commerce and confessed my sin.

The man replied, "Son, you are forgiven and as long as we didn't catch you, there is no way that we can fine you, but I must say, you are as strange as hair on a frog."

I have called other girls who God told me to call, but often they wouldn't even remember what I was confessing. Even then they would say, "Yes, I forgive you."

I got a letter recently from a girl who didn't remember the incident when I called to ask forgiveness, but has since then. She wrote how God used that phone call to get her back in fellowship with God. This is what she wrote:

Dear Fred,

I am not sure if I should write, because it may not be right, but it was the only way I could think of to thank you. For three or four years I haven't really cared about spiritual things and I've wandered about doing what I wanted to and making quite a mess! But the fact that after these years you called and asked forgiveness . . . it kind of spoke to me. So, thank you. Right now I'm in a Christian music group. . . . Well, I will go. I just

wanted to let you know that God used your phone call
to help me. Love,

Years had passed and she had forgotten, but the Spirit
of God faithfully poured conviction on my heart and
wanted this sin removed.

If Satan has a foothold in your moral life and if he is
always dragging you back into sexual sins, you need to
gain back the ground by asking forgiveness from those
whom you have offended. Until you do this ". . . you will
never get out till you have paid the last penny."

Speaking from experience, this is one of the most
difficult things this book asks you to do, but probably
the most important. To follow through and dial the
phone and say, "Will you forgive me for _____?"
will deeply humble you. As God points out those
you have sinned against remember these words;
"Humble yourselves therefore under the mighty
hand of God, that in due time He may exalt you"
(1 Peter 5:6).

Reviving the Soul

> The law of the LORD is perfect,
>> reviving the soul;
> the testimony of the LORD is sure,
>> making wise the simple;
> the precepts of the LORD are right,
>> rejoicing the heart;
> the commandment of the LORD is pure,
>> enlightening the eyes;

> the fear of the LORD is clean,
>> enduring for ever;
> the ordinances of the LORD are true,
>> and righteous altogether.
> More to be desired are they than gold,
>> even much fine gold;
> sweeter also than honey
>> and drippings of the honeycomb.

> Psalms 19:7–10

After this large step that Kimberly had taken, she was free from evil but she still needed some positive restoring of her soul. Tomorrow will be another day and she will need some inner strengthening for the future.

She came to me; once again we looked at the Bible together and I talked with her about one of the most healthy things anyone can ever do for himself . . . to memorize and meditate on Scripture.

"Kim, there are five very powerful things that the Word of God is used for: (1) It gives us discernment—". . . makes wise the simple," (2) It keeps our Christian lives exciting—". . . rejoicing the heart," (3) It gives us the ability to see things the way God sees them—". . . enlightening the eyes," (4) It gives us the fear of God—". . . the fear of the Lord is clean," (5) It makes us like Jesus—". . . and righteous altogether."

Now I could tell that she was catching on. "So, here's what to do, Kim, any Scripture would be good for you, but since you've had a weakness in this area, pick Scripture that would apply to this area of your life."

"Well, I really wouldn't know where to start. Do you have any suggestions?"

"Psalm 1 is always a good one to start off with. Just memorize it word for word. It emphasizes the real benefits of meditating, as well as comparing the righteous life with the wicked life. Then once you know it word for word, say it over and over again in your mind. Meditating really means murmuring because as the Jews would meditate, they would mumble the words of Scripture under their breath. It is also taken from the root word used in chewing the cud. Farmers say a cow chews the cud twenty-eight times, so we should say our verses over and over again."

Our conversation was rather one-sided and I never expected any results. However, since that day, Kim has memorized many other chapters on her own and has been reaping the benefits in her moral life. Every once in a while she will call and say, "Hey, Fred, I want to make you happy so I thought I'd call and let you know that I'm memorizing Psalm 113. Do you believe it, Fred? Me, memorizing all by myself? It is just fantastic!"

Kimberly was obedient to the voice of God and went from moral bondage to moral freedom. She was delivered from her sensuous desires, and her life is now fully under the Spirit's control. This is God's kind of freedom. This kind of freedom is made possible for everyone because of what Jesus Christ has done. If you are under moral bondage are you willing to follow the steps to total deliverance? (1) Come under your parents' authority. (2) Have a clean cut with sexual immorality.

(3) Burn the bridges behind you by asking forgiveness from those whom you have offended. (4) And lay up Scripture in your heart and thereby revive your soul. This may be the turning point in your life.

Right now get on your knees and say *yes* to God's Spirit and ask for His help in following through with each of these steps. It will not be the easiest route to take. As we have seen, there is a cost involved. But, Jesus told His disciples to count the cost before following Him (*see* Luke 14:25–33). If you desire to "do your own thing" in your life, don't pretend to be a follower of Another.

On the contrary, if you are willing to follow the biblical pattern of dating remember, "For God is at work within you, helping you want to obey him and then helping you do what he wants" (Philippians 2:13 LB). May God help you to follow in His steps.

7
Maintaining Freedom

... for God did not give us a spirit of timidity but
a spirit of power and love and self-control.

2 Timothy 1:7

Now that Kim has submitted to her parents and is
honoring them—now that she has cut herself off from
anyone with whom she would be involved immorally,
made her phone calls and gained forgiveness from her
past sins, and is actively reviving her soul through the
memorization and meditation of Scripture—she faces
the problems of holding on to the freedom that she has
gained.

All of us, whether we have to face an immoral past
or not, must face the daily tests of remaining pure in an
impure society. We all face temptation on television
and newsmagazines. The clothing styles and moral eth-
ics of our society are gnawing away at each one of us.
Perhaps the greatest pressure comes from that "friend"
who sits next to us in our first-period class who wants us
to join him in his sin.

I had one of these "friends" when I was in junior high
school. His name was Wayne. He had an older sister
who would always tell him the latest dirty jokes. In
turn, Wayne would always pass them along to me on

the school bus. He took me to my first *M*-rated movie and showed me many girlie magazines.

We didn't see each other for almost four years. The next time I saw him at a Fourth of July party, our lifestyles were entirely different. He was still looking at girlie magazines and getting into deeper sin, but I had found Jesus and He had cleaned me out. When we got together I was faced head on with a great temptation; was I going to show who I really was—a New Creation —or was I going to act as though I was the same old person?

The party continued for a couple of hours without any problems, then came the test. Roxanne sat down next to me and was acting rather silly. Soon she asked me if I would go upstairs to the bedroom and "make love" with her. Wayne was sitting next to me with a very attentive ear waiting for my answer. I'm sure he was terribly jealous that I was asked instead of him.

The real temptation that I faced was not whether or not to go to bed with her, because I wouldn't have done that, but the temptation was how to respond. Would I tell the real reason or would I make up some other excuse about "this other girl friend?"

Well, I told her something like this: "If I didn't know Jesus personally, I would be glad to go to bed with you." I didn't say that perhaps as softly as I should have and several others turned and looked at me as if I were some sort of a two-headed monster. I could never stand awkward moments so I filled in the long silence with a brief story of how I came to know Jesus Christ. Some of the people there were stoned, and it didn't effect them very much. However, it made quite an impact on those who were sober. In fact, at the end of a few minutes half the party was sitting around listening. When I thought that I was through, they asked for more. So I went on to tell them about healings and other stories of how God had been at work within me. What they previously thought was some sort of two-headed monster had now become a rather respectable, believable, Christian lifestyle. At this point I was very glad I had asked my mother to pray for me before I left the house that night.

That Fourth of July presented a test that not every Christian could handle, and I would not recommend getting yourself in a situation like that; however, we all face tests and threats to our life of moral purity and it is necessary for us to know how to handle these threats and how to protect and maintain our freedom. Here are a few suggestions as to how to protect that freedom.

"Along With Those Who Call Upon the Lord From a Pure Heart"

"Fleeing youthful passion" is not something that we are supposed to struggle with on our own. We are told in God's Word to protect our freedom ". . . along with those who call upon the Lord from a pure heart" (2 Timothy 2:22). I have seen too many people get sexually involved because they first became emotionally involved with a person who did not have a pure heart. Before we mentioned that it is harmful for a Christian to date a non-Christian, and however, it is even more harmful for a Christian to date another "Christian" who is morally impure.

Kim, who had gained total freedom, faced a terribly

difficult temptation because she became emotionally involved with a guy who did not have pure motives. It frightens me when I even recall the situation.

It was only two days ago when Kim first told Sherry and me about Frank. She had been witnessing to him about Jesus and he was very interested in God. She felt very sorry for him because he had been confined to bed for over a year, and his outside contacts had dwindled to nothing. Before she met Frank, she had told God that she would not date for quite a while—until He told her otherwise—but since Frank was confined to bed she decided to go to see him. Sherry and I thought nothing of it, but within a couple weeks she had "fallen" for him in an emotional way.

One night as Sherry and I were doing the dishes we worked our way into a rather hostile discussion. I even forget what it was about, but as I recall I was very harsh and overbearing. Satan had gained the advantage over our conversation and Sherry was in no position to take advice from me because of my insensitivity.

The phone rang and Sherry answered, "Oh, hi, Kim." Then silence. I immediately thought, "It must be that boy." As I prayed, Sherry offered comfort to a very confused teenager. As I overheard the conversation, I could tell what was going on. I prayed and God told me that it was a very desperate situation and that Satan was at work trying to destroy Kimberly's life. I desperately wanted to tell Sherry how to counsel Kim, but I couldn't. There was no way that I could give Sherry advice, because we were out of fellowship with each other. Satan had subtly gained the upper hand by causing a tiff between us in order to keep Kimberly from receiving wisdom from her spiritual authorities.

I just bowed my head and confessed my sin to Jesus and received His forgiveness. After Sherry hung up, I confessed to her, received her forgiveness, and then explained what had happened.

"Well, okay. Now that we are straightened out, what shall we do about Kim?" Sherry asked.

"Sherry, even though it sounds very innocent, God gave me a word of wisdom that she should not go to see him. In fact she should not even talk with him again." We went on discussing this for a while and I gave her several things to say to Kim, then Sherry called her back.

Sherry spoke the words God had given her to speak, and it was great. I could tell that God was ministering to Kim's heart. Sherry hung up a few minutes later, looked at me and said with huge eyes, "You won't believe it! You won't believe it! Frank just called her and told her that he wanted to have a sexual relationship with someone—and that someone would have been Kim! But, praise Jesus, Kim is going to be obedient to God's Word."

We were both amazed at the deceptiveness of Satan in coming between Sherry and me and trying to hinder our effectiveness in Kim's life, but we were even more amazed at how Satan was trying to use an impure boy to drag down a girl who had made a commitment to maintain purity.

This was Kimberly's trial. What is yours? No matter what it is, we need to protect ourselves by being with those with pure hearts. When I went to the Fourth of July party, I knew that it was going to present many temptations, so I asked my mother to pray for me that night—that God would keep me pure. When Kim was tempted by one who was not pure, she called two other Christians who were pure and she received strength and guidance from them. Before she called Frank to tell him *no* she said that she literally felt as though she was being dragged through hell. It was a very difficult decision for her to make, but she was faithful in maintaining purity.

Spending much time with someone (whether your own sex or the opposite sex) who is not pure is foolish. God warns us against it. Their language, life-style, thoughts, and their influence in our lives are not pure. This is why the Bible says, "Bad company ruins good morals" (1 Corinthians 15:33). We need to "shun youthful passions . . . along with those who call upon the Lord from a pure heart" (2 Timothy 2:22).

Dating is Not a Time for Evangelism

Kim found out that dating was not a time for evangelism, but almost had to suffer because she had great hopes of leading this boy to Jesus. He was a boy with impure motives and she was a girl with pure motives and they were just not going to make it. She described the pain that resulted from the tension as "hell."

I have led several girls to Jesus on dates and none of them ever grew in Jesus at all until I stopped dating them. And even then, many of them never continued with Jesus. There were too many emotional ties between us for the girl to truly be able to develop a love for Jesus independently of her affection for me.

God had been working in Helen's life for a few months through a Christian girl friend of hers, Brenda. I met Helen and was rather impressed with her so I asked her out. Well, one thing led to another and we began dating quite frequently. Even though we went to primarily church-related activities, although I talked about Jesus with her on just about every date, gave her a Bible and got her to read it every day, and she prayed and asked Jesus to come into her life one night on a date, God was not working in her life the way He wanted to. It would have been better if we were not dating.

We dated for a few months after her conversion, but neither one of us grew at all in Jesus. In fact, we both became less and less involved in church-related activities and with other Christians. Our relationship was pure, but it was having a negative effect on both of our spiritual lives. It was an "I'm in love with life" relationship.

We both agreed that it would be best if we stopped dating, so we did. She and Brenda became better friends, Helen was able to receive instruction and guidance from a more neutral source, and she became a more stable Christian.

I have since looked back on this example and thought how foolish and selfish it was for me to start dating Helen while God was using Brenda in her life. It would have been much better for all three of us if I had stayed out of the picture. If I really cared for Helen I would have wanted the best in her life, rather than selfishly wanting to date her.

Dating is not a ground for evangelism. Leading others to Jesus Christ is the most sacred activity we shall ever be involved in and it should not be confused with the shallow emotionalism of dating. Evangelism should be done within the sexes—boys to boys and girls to girls. If you are a girl and there is some boy that you really care about, do what Sally did.

Sally cared a lot about Brooks. However, she realized that she was not in the position to be used to lead him to salvation. So she told me about him first, and then she brought him to church on a Sunday night. As soon as the service was over I went down and talked with him. I knew that he was into football, as I had been, so we had a common ground. I found out he was a quarterback and since I was a receiver we had a lot to talk about. After a while I put the question at him, "Have you ever asked Jesus into your life?"

"No, I haven't."

"Would you mind if I told you what Jesus has done for you so that you can know God personally?"

"No, I don't mind," Brooks said matter-of-factly.

I opened to John 1 and took him through the first twelve verses. After I had told him the Good News I asked him, "If God is speaking to your heart, would you like to ask Jesus into your life right now?"

"Yes, I would."

"Well, let's pray right here. Let's get on our knees and either you can pray for yourself or I will pray and then you can repeat after me."

"I'll pray."

We were on our knees for almost thirty minutes while Sally was out in the church foyer jumping up and down holding my wife and screaming "Hallelujah" with all that she had.

For the next three months Brooks came under my discipleship and Sally never saw him except at church. She was earnestly praying for his growth and was showing tremendous Christian love for him by waiting on the sidelines. "Love is patient . . ." (1 Corinthians 13:4) as you recall. Then a few months later when Brooks had grown rapidly to a point of spiritual maturity, he began to ask Sally out, and they are growing beautifully together in Jesus.

Sally paid the price of waiting on God for His timing rather than trying to pick the fruit before it was ripe.

Avoid Certain Situations

> Can a man carry fire in his bosom
> and his clothes not be burned?
> Or can one walk upon hot coals
> and his feet not be scorched?
>
> Proverbs 6:27, 28

One of the things that Kim told me she learned after her trial with Frank was not to let herself get in a situation like that again. She should not have gone over to his house, called him up as often as she did, if at all, or allowed herself to think about him so much. She should not have become so emotionally involved. Kimberly recognized that what she was expressing to Frank was not agape love but possessiveness. Not Jesus, rather her own selfish desires.

Emotions can make slaves of young couples. During the dating stages of a boy-girl relationship it is most healthy to get to know one another mentally rather than emotionally, and certainly not physically. When Kim learned this she learned a very valuable principle.

There was a beautiful girl who I dated in high school. When I walked her to the door after the date to say good night, I totally froze, looked her in the face, but I couldn't say or do anything. So I turned away, got in my car and drove home. It was certainly embarrassing but I later realized what had happened. Because I was no different from any other red-blooded American male, I had desires at that moment other than merely saying good night. But God over-ruled. He caused my mind and body to jam up so all I could do was walk away. As I realized this on the way home all alone in the car, I laughed before the Lord with all my might. Since then, I have done this several times. Rather than doing something like kissing good night which would not have been appropriate I just walked away, shook hands in the car, or did something innocent like that.

When Calvin was getting "hot and heavy" one evening, Kim got up from watching T.V. and got a tall glass of milk. Later he wanted to spend the night at her house. Even though her parents would have been home and said it was okay, she knew that this would not be very wise. She insisted that he leave, even if his feelings would be hurt.

> Jesus said: "And if your hand causes you to sin, cut it off; it is better for you to enter life maimed than with two hands to go to hell, to the unquenchable fire. And if your foot causes you to sin, cut it off; it is better for you to enter life lame than with two feet to be thrown into hell. And if your eye causes you to sin, pluck it out; it is better for you to enter the kingdom of God with one eye than with two eyes to be thrown into hell, where their worm does not die, and the fire is not quenched.
>
> Mark 9:43–48

One of the most embarrassing things I have ever had to do on a date was to ask a girl to change her clothes because she was offending me with the short skirt that she wore. But it was either my eye or her skirt and I thought her skirt would be a lot less painful. I have since looked back on that incident and Proverbs 11:22 has come to mind, "Like a gold ring in a swine's snout, is a beautiful woman without discretion."

Being alone on a date is never a good idea. It is much better to be in a crowd. For obvious reasons, when you are in a crowd there are certain things that you will not be involved with. I am always concerned for the young people who always want to be alone with just their boy- or girl friend. Crowd activity always offers a much greater challenge to dating and is usually a lot more fun and creative.

When I was in high school our youth group did many social activities that were a lot of fun. However, there were always a few kids who had been dating for a long time who would go off alone. When I first met them they were very personable and friendly; however, after a year of dating one another, they withdrew from interaction with the other Christians and behaved very strangely. One boy later came to me confessing some very serious moral problems. This is certainly not the only cause, but it would have helped if they would not have been alone so much of the time. Crowd activities are much healthier for character and moral development.

Read the Bible Together

Reading the Word is one of the greatest things you can do together. It always amazes me when I realize the power in the Word of God. I know that the Bible says itself that it is " . . . living and active, sharper than any two-edged sword, piercing to the division of soul and spirit, of joints and marrow, and discerning the thoughts and intentions of the heart" (Hebrews 4:12), and yet I am always amazed.

God has taken Sherry and me on many different studies through the Word and yet every time He uncovers different areas of our lives which are in desperate need of help. One thing that always happens when we start a new study is that we become very irritable with each other. We get touchy, easily offended, selfish, defensive, and sinful in many other ways. After the first few times we read the Bible together we say, "If this is what happens when we read the Word together, are we sure that this is what God wants? Maybe we ought to do it alone and then compare notes."

Surprisingly, Sherry and I have had some of the greatest problems in our relationship as a result of studying the Bible. Even while we are talking about the verses that we have just read, we will speak very pridefully.

"I don't think it's saying that, I think it says this," Sherry will say.

"Hey, look. I'm the pastor in this family. I should know."

"Yes, Fred, you should know, but you don't."

"Hey, smarty-pants, if you don't watch out, I'm going to take my Bible and go home"—and on we go.

This only lasts for the first few days or even the first few minutes of a new Bible study, but the reason for it is because our flesh is being picked apart, so the old nature comes pouring out. Rather than exposing yourself to the potentially unrighteous effects of prayer, expose yourself to the righteous effects of reading God's Word.

There is nothing better that two people can do for each other than to hold each other accountable in Bible reading and meditating. This has definite eternal value. Jesus said, "Heaven and earth will pass away, but my words will not pass away" (Matthew 24:35).

Sherry and I met right before spring vacation and we

wanted our relationship to be in Jesus. Independently of each other, we decided to ask the Father what He wanted us to study from the Word that spring. I boarded my flight to Florida, opened my New Testament, and said, "Jesus, what is it that Sherry and I should read together?" Then I left it with Him. I opened to Ephesians and began reading. It was fantastic! The Spirit of God really ministered to my heart. I can remember reading from one of the first verses, "For consider what he has done—before the foundation of the world he chose us to be, in Christ, his children, holy and blameless in his sight" (Ephesians 1:4 PHILLIPS).

When I read that I said, "Yeah, that's what I want. I want Sherry and me to be your holy and blameless children living within your constant care." Through this and further reading during that week of vacation, God showed me that we were to read Ephesians.

When Sherry and I got back together again at Wheaton College, I asked her, "Did God direct you to a book?"

"I think so," she said timidly. "This past week there was a speaker who spoke at our church from the Book of Ephesians and God really spoke to me through it."

Bingo! Ephesians it was! We studied, God spoke, and all three of us had a fantastic time. Three nights a week we would get together in our student center, situate ourselves in a booth, and open our Bibles, concordances, and notebooks. In the next three months we worked our way through the first four chapters, keeping notes on all the insights which God gave us. We still have the notebook from that first study together. It wasn't the greatest study that has ever been done on the Book of Ephesians, but I would say it was the greatest thing we could have done together.

Through this, I saw how much God wants young adults to saturate their relationships with the Word of God. This first study that Sherry and I did gave our friendship roots in the righteous soil of God's love rather than in the unrighteous soil of our own egos.

Establish a Definite Moral Standard

> Cling tightly to your faith in Christ, and always keep your conscience clear, doing what you know is right. For some people have disobeyed their consciences and have deliberately done what they knew was wrong. It isn't surprising that soon they lost their faith in Christ after defying God like that.
>
> 1 Timothy 1:19 LB

The words, "Who says it's wrong," have led me and many others into sin. They are words from Satan himself. The serpent in Eden asked Eve, "Did God say ... ?" All Satan has to do is get us to reject our consciences and he has led us into acts of disobedience.

There was a girl in our freshman class at college who had lived a very sheltered life and had never established a moral standard. A boy took her out on a date with the expressed purpose of seeing how much he could get off her. They went out, he made some moves, and the girl lowered herself to his level. For the next two years of college this left scars upon her conscience. She had never been taught what was right or wrong, but she knew in her conscience that she had done wrong.

It is very important for everyone to establish a definite biblically based moral standard that will not be lowered even if it means losing dates. Rather than making hand-holding white and intercourse black and everything else in between grey, we need to draw a definite line. The definite moral standard will protect us against the pull of our lower nature at weak moments.

Today, many Christian young people have never had God's moral standards made clear to them, and as a result, fall to temptations. For this reason, everyone must establish his own standards, based upon the Word of God and his conscience. It is helpful to vow to keep that standard even if it means losing certain "friends." Until such a standard is set, you are not ready to date.

"Resist the Devil and He Will Flee From You"

Satan, the enemy of our souls, is roaming around seeking to swallow committed disciples of the Lord Jesus Christ like you and me. He just loves to have us lust after someone and dwell on immoral thoughts. He would just love us to challenge God's Word and disobey what the Lord Jesus has told us to do.

When Kim was going through terrible temptations and times of real depression and confusion, she called and asked for a little advice.

"Hey, Kim, I want you to read Romans 5 and 6; Gala-

tians 5; 1 Thessalonians 4; and Psalm 119. Ask Jesus for
a verse—no, two verses—to memorize. Then, all day
tomorrow quote those verses to yourself whenever
your thoughts start to wander."

"I can't do that."

"Why not?" I asked.

"I'll be saying those verses all day long."

"That's right, Kim, you're catching on."

She laughed and said, "Okay, okay."

The next afternoon I got a call. It was Kim. "Fred, it
was a great day."

"Did those verses come in handy?"

"No, they weren't any good at all."

I thought to myself, "Oh, no."

"But God gave me two other ones that I said all day
long. He really brought my mind under control."

We praised God for the victory that He won over
Satan in Kim's mind.

In Matthew 4 Satan tempted Jesus and the weapon
that Jesus used against him was the Word of God—
Scripture. In Ephesians 6 we read about the weapons
of our warfare; the sword of the Spirit—the Word of
God—is the only offensive weapon. All the others are
defensive. God expects us to answer back to Satan
when he lies to us. The Bible says that " . . . When he
lies, he speaks according to his own nature, for he is a
liar and the father of lies" (John 8:44).

Satan spoke through Peter to Jesus and Jesus said,
"Get behind me Satan." Satan can use other people to
speak lies to us also. We need to be full of wisdom and
discernment and rebuke the devil with the Word of

God whenever he comes truckin' across our path.

I went to a coed college where there were a large percentage of good-looking and rather shapely females. I would walk a mile to and from campus every day and God gave me a Scripture that I could quote as I would walk along the street. Whenever a long leg or rather pronounced curves walked by I would silently say, "How can a young man keep his way pure? By guarding it according to thy word" (Psalm 119:9). I would even act out the verse. As I would walk along, and see someone, I would literally stop, turn, hold up my fist as if I had a shield in one hand and a sword in another, and say, "How can a young man like me keep his way pure? By guarding it according to thy word!"

Once, while sitting in a literature class, I went through these same motions because the girl across the room was improperly dressed. I thrust my sword with such a definite gesture that I interrupted the professor's train of thought and had half the class wondering if I was having a seizure. The only seizure that was taking place was that the Lord Jesus was seizing the devil and calling him a liar. I didn't care what they thought. I was free and God was glorified.

Resisting Satan is usually a very simple process but few Christians actually understand how this is done:

Step 1:   Recognize the Tempter
          We can be certain Satan is tempting us when our thoughts are in direct contradiction to what we know is God's will.
Step 2:   Submit yourself to God

We need to consciously pray, "God, I give myself to You—I am Yours" (*see* James 4:7).

Step 3: Quote a verse of Scripture to Satan, such as: "Satan, I rebuke you in the name of the Lord Jesus Christ, for it is written. . . ."

Step 4: Praise God for the Victory (*see* Hebrews 3:14 and Colossians 2:15).

There are many verses which I have memorized since then. The Word of God is our only offensive weapon in dealing with the devil and we need to memorize as many verses as we possibly can. We should each ask Jesus which verses are the sharpest weapons for us to use. Everyone is different and everyone needs to choose different swords. Here are a few which have been helpful to me.

In a great house there are not only vessels of gold and silver but also of wood and earthenware, and some for noble use, some for ignoble. If anyone purifies himself from what is ignoble, then he will be a vessel for noble use, consecrated and useful to the master of the house, ready for any good work. So shun youthful passions and aim at righteousness, faith, love, and peace, along with those who call upon the Lord from a pure heart.

2 Timothy 2:20–22

Jesus gave these to me to memorize at a time of great temptation. I decided that He wanted me to be involved in some sort of ministry. If I was going to spend my whole life in His service, I wasn't going to settle for anything but the best just because of some raunchy thoughts. The Master of the house places His vessels— you and me—where He choses, so we had better "shun youthful passions."

Here are a few more helpful swords.

> How can a young man keep his way pure?
>   By guarding it according to thy word.
> I have laid up thy word in my heart,
>   that I might not sin against thee.
>
> Psalms 119:9, 11

You have heard that it was said, "You shall not commit adultery." But I say to you that everyone who looks at a woman lustfully has already committed adultery with her in his heart. If your right eye causes you to sin, pluck it out and throw it away; it is better that you lose one of your members than that your whole body be thrown into hell.

Matthew 5:27–29

For sin will have no dominion over you, since you are not under law but under grace.

Romans 6:14

There is therefore now no condemnation for those who are in Christ Jesus.

Romans 8:1

Shun immorality. Every other sin which a man commits is outside the body; but the immoral man sins against his own body. Do you not know that your body is a temple of the Holy Spirit within you, which you have from God? You are not your own; you were bought with a price. So glorify God in your body.

1 Corinthians 6:18–20

For freedom Christ has set us free; stand fast therefore, and do not submit again to a yoke of slavery.

Galatians 5:1

But I say, walk by the Spirit, and do not gratify the desires of the flesh. For the desires of the flesh are against the Spirit, and the desires of the Spirit are against the flesh; for these are opposed to each other, to prevent you from doing what you would.

Galatians 5:16, 17

All those who belong to Christ Jesus have crucified the flesh with its passions and desires.

Galatians 5:24

Do not be deceived; God is not mocked, for whatever a man sows, that he will also reap. For he who sows to his own flesh will from the flesh reap corruption; but he who sows to the Spirit will from the Spirit reap eternal life. And let us not grow weary in welldoing, for in due season we shall reap, if we do not lose heart.

Galatians 6:7–9

God's plan is to make you holy, and that means a clean cut with sexual immorality. Every one of you should learn to control his body, keeping it pure and treating it with respect, and never allowing it to fall victim to lust, as do pagans with no knowledge of God. You cannot break this rule without cheating and exploiting your fellow-men. Indeed God will punish all who do offend in this matter, as we have plainly told you and warned you. The calling of God is not to impurity but the most thorough purity, and anyone who makes light of the matter is not making light of man's ruling but of God's command. It is not for nothing that the Spirit God gives us is called the Holy Spirit.

1 Thessalonians 4:3–8 PHILLIPS

The ultimate aim of the Christian ministry, after all, is to produce the love which springs from a pure heart, a good conscience and a genuine faith.

1 Timothy 1:5 PHILLIPS

. . . for God did not give us a spirit of timidity but a spirit of power and love and self-control.

2 Timothy 1:7

I write to you, young men, because you are strong, and the word of God abides in you, and you have overcome the evil one.

1 John 2:14b

Since this is verse 24 of Jude, I always say it gives me round-the-clock protection:

> Now to him who is able to keep you from falling and to present you without blemish before the presence of his glory with rejoicing . . . be glory. . . .

These have been very beneficial in my life as I have sought to maintain the freedom that Jesus has provided me with. They have been the joy and rejoicing of my heart. The list can go on and on but I trust that the Spirit of God will direct your heart to claim some verses for your own personal use.

Make this your prayer. "Father, I do desire to walk in newness of life. Keep me mindful of these various methods of maintaining freedom. Praise You, Jesus."

8
Newfound Energy

> Let not sin therefore reign in your mortal bodies,
> to make you obey their passions. Do not yield your
> members to sin as instruments of wickedness, but
> yield yourselves to God as men [and women] who
> have been brought from death to life, and your mem-
> bers to God as instruments of righteousness. For sin
> will have no dominion over you, since you are not
> under law but under grace.
>
> Romans 6:12-14

After a few days of real spiritual victory in my life, I
was sitting in our college library studying Greek. There
is nothing more threatening to spiritual highs than
Greek grammar. Due to the fact that my mind would
rather do just about anything than concentrate on
Greek, it was easy to notice a few legs and curves moving by.

"Hold it. Thoughts, stay right where you are. I refuse
to let you do that."

Then Satan got into the picture. "Aw, take another
look. There's nothing wrong with that. Go ahead."

I rebuked Satan: "In the name of the Lord Jesus
Christ, I rebuke you, Satan, for He has said, '. . . be holy,
for I am holy'" (Leviticus 11:44). Satan immediately

fled, but my thoughts and desires were not pure. This bothered me so I asked God for help and His Spirit said, "Open to Matthew 5." I did and I read about how lust of the eye was no less offensive to God than adultery. I was hurting.

"I agree, God. I know it's wrong. I know I must control my thoughts. But how?" I sat there trying desperately, but I couldn't.

"Will you trust me?" the Spirit of God asked.

"Yes," I quickly answered.

"Open to Romans 5." I obeyed immediately and read through into chapter 6. It was all good, but then I saw it. It was as if the Spirit of God took the scales off my eyes and gave me a truth that I would rely on through the years ahead. One, two, three, and then the promise! Praise God.

The *first* thing He showed me was in verse 4:

> We were buried therefore with him by baptism into death, so that as Christ was raised from the dead by the glory of the Father, we too might walk in newness of life.
>
> Romans 6:4

This is the statement of truth: "We were buried with him." Even though I certainly didn't feel as though I was buried with Christ, it was nonetheless true.

The *second* thing that He showed me was in verse 11:

So you also must consider yourselves dead to sin and
alive to God in Christ Jesus.

Romans 6:11

Not only did He die, and I with Him, but I needed to
consider this true for myself. While I was sitting there
in the library with less than pure desires, I needed to
consider myself dead to sin. I needed to affirm before
God that those desires that my flesh was producing
were actually coming from a dead man. They were
"leftovers," so to speak.

The *third* thing that God showed me to do was in
verse 13:

Do not yield your members to sin as instruments of
wickedness, but yield yourselves to God as men who
have been brought from death to life, and your members to God as instruments of righteousness.

Romans 6:13

Since I was dead with Jesus and alive in Jesus, I could
yield my thoughts to whatever I wanted; either to sin
or to God. Right there in the library I bowed my head
and said, "Jesus, I thank You that I died with You and
that I don't have to sin against You in my thought life.
Right now I yield myself to You as a new creature." I
lifted my head, smiled, and praised God.

Then I looked down at the page and read the next
verse, verse 14, which was to become one of my favorite
promises: "For sin will have no dominion over you,

since you are not under law but under grace" (Romans 6:14).

After I went through that three-step process I knew that I was no longer a slave to sin, but it was great to have God tell me. One, two, three, and then the promise, praise God!

Jesus said, "You shall know the truth and the truth shall set you free." The truth is that we have died with Christ Jesus. This is the greatest truth we will ever be able to claim, as far as channeling lustful desires is concerned.

I found this to be so exciting that I went on to tell many of the other brothers on campus, and it was very helpful to them also. The most fascinating thing about this process is that after these desires have been laid hold of and channeled, they give off fantastic spiritual energy. I found myself just eating up Scripture, wanting to share Jesus with others who didn't yet know Him, and even studying Greek grammar. But, it wasn't until recently that I have discovered why this energy is produced.

A few days ago, while I was reading through a magazine, some lustful thoughts were suddenly triggered within me. I panicked. "Oh, no. What shall I do?" I rebuked them, but they were still there. I confessed them and received His forgiveness, but they were still there. I got desperate and asked Him, "Father, what shall I do?"

He answered very quietly, "Praise Me for them."

"Praise You? God, You don't understand. These are lustful thoughts and desires. What do You really want me to do?"

"Praise Me." The words came back again.

So, I did something I have never done before. I praised Him for those raunchy thoughts. As I began to praise Him, I experienced a tremendous flow of the Holy Spirit. I was freed from any further lust throughout that day. I was greatly empowered to get more work done than I ever could have ordinarily, and God was abundantly glorified.

God is able to lay hold of even our lustful desires and transform them, thereby bringing glory to Himself. The Bible says that desire gives birth to sin. However, desire is not sin! (*See* James 1:14, 15.) If God can gain the upper hand in our own personal desires a tremendous level of spiritual energy can be tapped.

I have led several people to Jesus as a result of channeling my sexual desires into a godly motivation. I read through the Bible last year with tremendous enthusiasm and hunger because my sexual desires were properly channeled. In one month this past summer I zealously taught or preached the Word thirty times as a result of yielding my sex life to Jesus Christ and sublimating physical drives into spiritual avenues.

I don't say this to in any way boast of my personal achievements, because there are men and women around the world who have far exceeded any success that I have had. However, they, too, have tapped the power source! What contributes to making a dynamic evangelist, church worker, soul winner, or preacher is a totally yielded sex life to the Lordship of Jesus Christ. We each need to release these energies in holy creativity.

If ye then be risen with Christ, seek those things which
are above, where Christ sitteth on the right hand of
God. Set your affections on things above, not on things
on the earth. For ye are dead, and your life is hid with
Christ in God.

Colossians 3:1–3 KJV

As most of us have discovered, we cannot always
suppress sexual desires as if we were putting our finger
in a dike. God does not expect us to set our affections
on nothing and turn into some sort of subhuman being.
When we become Christians, we are completely re-
deemed: body, soul, and spirit, and this includes our sex
lives. We don't get rid of our sexual desires as Christians. In fact, as Christians our sex drives are purified
and strengthened. The sex drives of a Christian should
be stronger than any non-Christian's because in Christ
we are growing up to mature manhood (*see* Ephesians
4:13), and manhood partially means sexuality. Therefore, as Christians we have much greater resources of
energy to channel into service, dedication, and zeal for
the Lord Jesus Christ. As Paul writes, "For you were
called to freedom, brethren; only do not use your freedom as an opportunity for the flesh, but through love
be servants of one another" (Galatians 5:13). This verse
makes the options very plain: either living for the flesh
or living to serve others. This same concept is restated
in 1 Peter 4:2, ". . . so as to live for the rest of the time
in the flesh no longer by human passions but by the will
of God."

The "how to's" of changing sexual desires into spiritual activity are really very simple. Here's how it's done. . . .

Acknowledge the Lustful Desires

When lustful thoughts come crawling across our minds it is very easy to try to deny them or hide from them. When passions are aroused within us we might panic and desperately feel that we have been defeated. However, God intends to use these drives for His purpose. They should not be dismissed or immediately discarded. As James writes, "When all kinds of trials and temptations crowd into your lives, my brothers, don't resent them as intruders, but welcome them as friends!" (James 1:2 PHILLIPS).

As I sat in the Wheaton College library, I tried desperately to fight off those fleshly desires, but I failed. I sat as a defeated Christian. But when I faced up to them, when I agreed with God that my thoughts were lustful, I placed myself in a position where the Spirit of God was able to minister to me. So each of us needs to say, "Yes, God. I agree. I am a sinner. These thoughts and desires that I have are certainly lustful and raunchy in Your sight. I agree with You and humble myself before You."

Rebuke the Devil

As was laid out in the previous chapter, Scripture is our only offensive weapon against the lies of the devil. The way that we need to rebuke the devil is to confront him head-on in the Name of the Lord Jesus Christ and quote a verse "Thus saith the Lord. . . ." If Satan comes truckin' along and says to me, "It's a lot of fun to think about that girl, isn't it? Go ahead, you have no other choice," I will come back immediately with a rebuke: "Satan, I command you in the Name of the Lord Jesus Christ to flee from me. It is written, 'Sin has no more dominion over you, since you are not under the law but under grace.'"

We need to gain control over our thoughts, rather than yield them over to the devil. Our thoughts and desires must be brought under the control of the truth of God's Word . . . after all, "How can a young man keep his way pure? By guarding it according to thy word."

Praise God for This Power and Energy

Once we have brought our desires under God's control, we can praise Him for them. James tells us ". . . to welcome them as friends" or "Count it all joy. . . ." That afternoon as I was reading through the magazine with lustful desires I could hardly believe my ears when God said, "Praise ME for them." "What good could they possibly be?" I questioned. I think that this is part of what Paul meant when he wrote, "I can even enjoy weaknesses, insults, privations, persecutions and diffi-culties for Christ's sake. For my very weakness makes me strong in him" (2 Corinthians 12:10 PHILLIPS).

In the same way Jesus wants us to redirect our natural reactions to lustful desires—frustration or defeat—and rather say, "Thank You, Jesus, for this desire. I know

You have a purpose for it in my life."

As I've mentioned, when I began to praise God for the desires within me, the Spirit of God flowed through me in a marvelous way and I was aware of a new incentive to eagerly do God's will in my life. My praising gave God the freedom He desired to work His will through me.

Ask Him How He Wants You to Spend This New Energy

"God, this power is fantastic, but what's it for? Do You want me to pray with zeal? Do You want me to read the Bible with enthusiasm? Do You want me to do what my parents asked me to do a few days ago (mow the lawn, take out garbage, and so forth)? Do that homework assignment that I put off for three weeks? Write those friends?" There are a score of very positive activities that God intends for us to use our energies on.

When Sherry and I first started dating, we had our share of sexual desires to account for. We were aware of the dangers, but God gave us a very creative assignment.

I had always been used to a lot of physical exercise in high school, and in intermural sports in the fall and winter at college. But now it was spring and there was nothing to do. As Sherry and I would walk across campus I would feel like crawling out of my skin because I was so attracted to her. My thoughts were not all lustful, but I had all this energy and nothing to do with it. One afternoon as we got to the dorm she went to her room and I went to mine.

The phone rang, "Hi, let's play tennis," Sherry suggested.

"What a great idea. Why didn't I think of it?" In the cool of the afternoon we went out and played a lousy game of tennis. But it was fun; it was good exercise and very refreshing. The next day we went jogging and continued exercising through the spring quarter. It was a very positive activity and we burned off a lot of excess passion and desire.

As I have previously mentioned, we also engaged in a very productive Bible study in the Book of Ephesians. Rather than just going out for evening walks, we got together around the Word of God. With all the extra motivation, we planted our relationship in the righteous soil of God's Word. I had never gotten so many insights into the Word before that time. Sherry really thought that I was a spiritual giant (and I didn't tell her any differently, either).

I pray for you, my brother or sister, that through this chapter you will hear God's voice instructing you in righteousness and that the Holy Spirit will be at work within you, ". . . giving you the will and the power to achieve his purpose" (Philippians 2:13b PHILLIPS). God desires to continue to transform our sexual drives into spiritual energy. He wants us to continue to set our affections on things above: to love Jesus obsessively, until we all gather together at that great marriage supper of the Lamb.

9
Now Am I Ready to Date?

But seek ye first the kingdom of God, and his righteousness; and all these things shall be added unto you.

Matthew 6:33 KJV

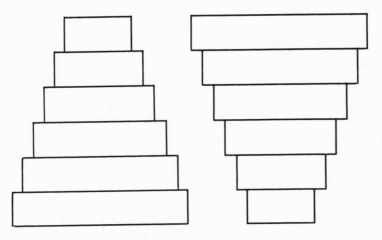

Which of the above constructions is more stable?

One of the most difficult parts of the Christian life is keeping our priorities straight. When other interests crowd into our lives it is very easy to give the important things a back seat.

When Jesus used the parable of the sower he explained how the seed that sprang right up and was choked out by thorns was representative of the person who hears the Gospel and responds to it, then some time in the near future other interests gain greater priority in the person's life (*see* Mark 4:19).

Unfortunately, dating can cause great mix-ups in our Christian lives. Our parents, schoolwork, other Christians, our outreach, and even God Himself can gradually get squeezed into the background because some girl catches our attention.

When priorities assume their proper perspective, however, dating can help to deepen a young Christian's life in a beautiful way. Let's look at the following six priorities in order of importance to God.

Priority One: God

> . . . you shall love the LORD your God with all your heart, and with all your soul, and with all your might.
>
> Deuteronomy 6:5

The first sure sign of an unhealthy relationship is that at least one of the two people is growing less interested in God.

Cindy was never a really dynamic Christian, but she nevertheless had a sincere love for God. She met Him at a Billy Graham movie and got quite involved in a Campus Life Club in Illinois. The club was a large one of around one hundred fifty students, and things were quite exciting. She was a very active leader of the club until she met Kenny.

Cindy's mother noticed a change in her whole personality when they met each other, but the most drastic change was that she apparently lost all interest in the things of God. No more church or Campus Life, no more Bible reading, prayer, fellowship with other Christians, and no more of a lot of other things. Cindy had lost interest, and the seed of the Gospel apparently was being choked out because of her newfound interest in Kenny. She became practically obsessed with him, and they spent all their time with each other. They would go to football games, concerts, road rallies, drive-ins, and so forth. Everything was go, go, go, and she was quite swept along with it all.

This example could have been a lot of other people too. I'm sure we have all seen, if not been personally involved, in a situation just like this one. However, God has a better idea!

God says, "Seek ye first the Kingdom of God. . . ." and "love me with all your heart. . . ." and "set your affections on things above, not on things on the earth. . . ." God wants our undivided attention to be primarily on Him and everything else is to be secondary. Remember He warns us: "Do not lay up for yourselves treasures on earth where romances can grow cold and I.D. bracelets can be returned, or where Don Juans can break in and steal affections."

Fortunately, Cindy's story has a happy ending (unlike several others I could have told). It took several years of prayer and patience on the part of God and her family, but the Spirit of God convicted her of her waywardness and sinful independence.

One day Kenny came over and he found her reading the Bible. I'm sure he smelled the trouble brewing. He tried to distract her, but it was no use. She insisted that they start reading the Bible together every time they got together. (At this point, Kenny couldn't have cared less about Jesus. In fact he never did.) For a few weeks he stuck it out with much grumbling, and then it was all over. Kenny wasn't fighting against Cindy; this time it was against God. From that day on Jesus got ahold of Cindy in a beautiful way and has been conforming her to His image ever since. She is now very active in living for Him. He is her Number One priority.

The place that God wants each one of us to protect is our time alone with Him . . . our private communion. This is where He started with Cindy and this is what He desires with each one of us. We feel free enough to keep secrets with close friends and these secrets deepen our relationship. So it is with God. When we keep secrets with Him, our relationship with Him is strengthened. Jesus tells us, " 'But when you pray, go into your room, and shut the door and pray to your Father who is in secret; and your Father who sees in secret will reward you" (Matthew 6:5). We have got to protect our private communion from the attacks of outside interests.

God also desires our thought lives to be stayed on Him.

Billy-Jo is a beautiful girl. She was chosen out of a large number to be in a beauty contest. Because of this she gained quite an interest among the male population, and she knew it. She began to think too much about herself and her reputation. She came to me, explained the situation, and asked for some advice. I quoted her the verse, "Thou wilt keep him in perfect peace, whose mind is stayed on thee: because he trusteth in thee" (Isaiah 26:3 KJV). I went on to give her a verse to quote whenever she began to think about herself rather than about the Lord: ". . . man looks on the outward appearance, but the LORD looks on the heart" (1 Samuel 16:7). She later told me what a blessing it was to her. She memorized it and quoted it during the beauty contest.

"I couldn't believe what joy bubbled up in my heart whenever I quoted those verses. And the peace . . . wow! It was really beautiful." She went on to tell me how she had previously thought a lot about what "the guys" were thinking about her but now she had a very positive way to control her thoughts.

There is one very practical way to assure ourselves that God will always be the Number One priority in our lives . . . we need to constantly be placing the "Kennys" on the altar.

Abraham waited a long time for a son. When he finally and miraculously got one, God asked him to do an amazing thing: "He said, 'Take your son, your only son Isaac, whom you love, and go to the land of Moriah, and offer him there as a burnt offering upon one of the mountains of which I shall tell you.' " Then Abraham did an amazing thing: "So Abraham rose early in the morning, saddled his ass . . . and went to the place of which God had told him" (Genesis 22:2, 3). We are probably all familiar with this story in Genesis but it sets forth a vital dating and life principle.

God doesn't have to ask us to place the things we don't care for on the altar. We automatically place those in the trash heap. It's the things or people we love that He asks us to place on the altar. It's those areas of our lives which we really dig on, like "that new girl" we just met or "that guy with the Vet" we've been going out with for a few weeks. That's the one God wants.

Very early in my friendship with Sherry, God taught us something that I had never been asked to do before. We were talking together and He spoke to me, "Give her to Me." It sounded like the craziest idea I could imagine, but I was obedient. This one time I thought praying together was okay. So I started, "God, Sherry is Yours. I know You want her. If I never see her again, it's okay because she is all Yours. Amen." I was afraid to open my eyes to look at Sherry. Finally I got up enough guts and I did it. I couldn't believe it. She had tears in her eyes and she said, "That was beautiful." Then she proceeded to pray a very similar prayer. This set a great pattern for our relationship and we have continued doing this until this very day. It has protected our love from getting covetous or fleshly and has rooted us in the soil of Jesus Christ Himself.

The problem that Cindy faced was not Kenny. Very often parents, particularly mothers, come to me and tell some long story about how "this other boy" or "the crowd" has caused their child to wander away from Jesus. I usually try to be sympathetic, and I am truly sorry that there is a spiritual breakdown in their child, but I never believe that it is "So-and-so's" fault. Cindy caused her own problems. The breakdown in her life was not to be blamed on Kenny. It really revealed a weakness in Cindy's life. She suffered from a break-down in priorities, and when she set her priorities straight, Kenny didn't present any further problem to her and the atmosphere became so uncomfortable for him that he left. The best way to remove thorns and thistles from a healthy garden is to have thriving plants. As Cindy placed Kenny on God's altar and began to thrive in Jesus the thorns in her life were crowded out.

Jesus said, "No one of you can be my disciple who does not give up all of his possessions" (*see* Luke 14:33). If there is anything between ourselves and Jesus we need to lay it on the altar of God; not just today, but today, and the next day, and the next. If there is some-one special in your life right now make this your prayer: "Jesus, You are Lord of my life, and that includes my dating life. Right now I place ——— on the altar. He/she is in Your hands. Whether we ever see each other again or not is up to You because my hope is in You. Thanks."

Priority Two: Family

> Children, obey your parents in the Lord, for this is right. "Honor your father and mother" (this is the first commandment with a promise), "that it may be well with you, and that you may live long on the earth."
>
> Ephesians 6:1–3.

It is very easy to let the parents slip down the list of priorities until we can hardly remember what they look like, and the parents feel like asking what my dad did,

"Hey, Fred! When can I *have* a *date* with you?" This is the second breakdown that can be caused by dating too seriously, the family breakdown.

One of the ways that this breakdown can take place is when the guy tries to get the girl to submit as if he owned her. I have often seen some guys (including myself) act as if they really possessed the girl like a squaw. There are also certain girls with the "blow in my ear and I'll follow you anywhere" philosophy who are just waiting for that prince charming to come along and sweep her off her feet. She'll get his ring or bracelet of security and act as if she's ready to retire socially. These relationships are ugly, stifling, and harmful.

A girl is never to submit to a guy until she gets married. A girl's full submission is to be directed toward her parents and anything that interrupts this divine order is a demonic counterfeit and will at least temporarily stop the working of God in a young person's life.

I know several girls whose parents insist that any interested boy receive their permission before their daughter can go out with him. This is perfectly godly. It probably sounds weird if you've never heard it before, but that's because man didn't think of it. God did. If the parents aren't to be asked by the boy, the girl should definitely check with the parents before every date.

Let me tell you a story that ought to make your hair stand on end.

When I was in grammar school I was one of the tallest kids in my class. During soccer season I was the goalie on the team and this brought quite a bit of recognition among the older students, particularly among the female population. There was one girl who was new to the neighborhood, and all the guys had their eyes on her. Her name was Ramona. She had brown hair and was quite good-looking. All the others were after her, but for some strange reason she got a crush on me. All my friends were telling me to call her up and ask her out. I was pretty slow with the girls and had never really called anyone on the phone before. I felt quite nervous about the whole situation.

I was pacing around the house for hours until I finally got up enough guts. As I dialed the phone my mother came walking in and asked, "What are you doing?"

"Shhh! I'll tell you in a minute. I'm calling Ramona right now."

The line was busy and as I hung up my mother came in, sat on my bed, and explained that she didn't think that I should call her, go out with her, or get close to her in any way. She had met Ramona at one of my soccer games and got some "woman's intuition" or something. I didn't exactly understand what she was talking about, but I obeyed. So, I explained it to my friends and I never got to know Ramona.

Before long, rumors started to circulate about Ramona's moral life. By the time I graduated from high school she had to get married and has since that day been divorced and remarried several times.

How my mother knew what Ramona was like I'll never know, but God used her guidance to steer me away from a pit of the devil. Because of my innocence there was no way that God could have saved me except through the instruction of a concerned mother, and it was fortunate that I was obedient.

Not long ago Tammy's mom called Sherry. She was all upset. "Tammy has always been so open and honest with me, but since she's been dating Toni it seems as though we can't talk about anything. I just know that they are up to no good."

Sherry knew exactly what the problem was because we had suspected some moral problems. There wasn't much Sherry could say but she assured the mother of her prayer support. After she hung up, Sherry and I prayed for Tammy and her mother. A week later Sherry asked Tammy how she was getting along with her mom. "Oh, wow! Much better. Now that Toni and I are straightened out, things are back to normal." She went on to tell Sherry about all the problems she and her mother were facing, thinking that Sherry was learning something new. At the time Sherry left the issue, but has since been able to instruct Tammy about the importance of open communication between parents and children.

Parents are a much greater priority than even "that special someone." We need to always keep them in their God-given place, constantly seek their counsel, and keep the channels of communication open.

Jan's parents didn't give her much advice so she would always come to Sherry and me for counsel. We are serving as her spiritual parents until her mom and dad become Christians. This chain of counsel is certainly secondary to her parents' advice, but it has been very helpful to Jan in areas where her parents give her no guidance at all.

If you do not have parents who will give you counsel in your dating life, ask God to direct you to a spiritual mother or father. If you have parents who offer advice (perhaps too much sometimes), it might be helpful for you to pray this prayer: "I praise You, Father, for my parents. I praise You for the way You speak to me through them. I praise You for their love and concern for me and for the wisdom they have given me. I submit to it, and by Your grace will be obedient to it. Praise You, Father!"

Priority Three: Government

> Let every person be subject to the governing authorities. For there is no authority except from God, and those that exist have been instituted by God. Therefore he who resists the authorities resists what God has appointed, and those who resist will incur judgment. For rulers are not a terror to good conduct, but to bad. Would you have no fear of him who is in authority? Then do what is good, and you will receive his approval.
>
> Romans 13:1–3

Both going to school and holding a job are to be given higher priority than "that special someone." Both teachers and employers are God-given authorities and as long as we are in subjection to them, we are to hold them up as a priority. Dating can very definitely cause a breakdown at this level.

When Sherry and I first went out, it was as if I was

taking an added twelve-hour course, and my grades showed it. Although we were involved in healthy activities, we were to some extent overinvolved. Sherry had great discipline in her studies at that time and she could handle it, but I was thrown all out of whack. I'll never forget the first exam week after we met each other . . . terrible.

I was to have three exams on the final day of the quarter—philosophy, psychology, and sociology—they were all in the morning, back to back. That week I averaged three hours sleep a night and went two nights without any at all. Besides the tests I had two term research papers to complete with a total of forty-five pages. I can assure you that the day of my exams I floated from one test to the next. Everyone was asking me if I felt all right and later Sherry told me that my breath was horrendous! Needless to say, my grades were not the greatest in the world: three *C*'s were the worst of my college career. I knew something was wrong and God showed me what it was.

The next quarter things were different and I was on the honor role, just as Sherry was. God taught me (the hard way) that our education was to take higher priority than our relationship.

One weekend there was a concert that we were looking forward to for a long time. There was one problem: Sherry had a book review due on Monday and she hadn't even read the book yet.

"That's easy," I told her. "I read that lousy book twice when I was in high school. I'll help you with it in the afternoon and then we can go to the concert." She agreed and we were in business.

We started early in the morning and worked faithfully and steadily. We outlined the whole paper. I thought of a great opening sentence and got her well on the way. She spent the rest of the afternoon writing and we were both very impressed with how disciplined we had become in giving our studies a higher priority. We were even able to make it to the concert that Saturday night because we did first things first.

An amazing thing happened when we walked into the professor's office a week later to pick up the paper. It was an easy *A,* we were convinced. Sherry walked in to get it while I waited outside. I didn't even have to look at the front of it, I knew what she got. It was the best paper I had ever written and the opening sentence was sensational; just a terrific outline. As we walked out I caught a glance at Sherry's face. She was crying. I looked down at the paper and the thing looked like it was bleeding. There was a big *C* on the front with red marks all over the place. I read what it said, "Poor opening sentence. Disunity, poor flow. . . ." We looked at each other, I threw my arms around her and we laughed our heads off. "I don't care what he says. That was the best paper I ever wrote."

Despite the poor grade that Sherry got we were learning, and we were seeking to give our studies their rightful priority.

Another couple at college with Sherry and me was Julie and Dan. They set a fantastic example for all of us. Dan was studying premed and had quite a future of schooling in front of him. They both realized this, and even though they were both very active socially, they purposed to help each other keep their schooling before their relationship. Dan was a cocaptain of the football team his senior year, and this cut back even further on the time that they could spend with each other in the fall. When they graduated, Dan was admitted into the medical school of his choice and they were married midway through the summer. Now they can spend all the time that they want together. Dan put his schooling as well as his vocation before Julie, and the Spirit of God was able to lead him effectively. Today they are reaping the benefits.

Schooling and employment need to be given greater priority than dating. Peace and real stability will remain in a relationship which guards this priority, as Julie and Dan found out.

Priority Four: The Body of Christ

" . . . not neglecting to meet together, as is the habit of some, but encouraging one another, and all the more as you see the Day drawing near"

(Hebrews 10:25)

That "special someone" can cause a breakdown in the family of God just as he or she can in our human families.

The first date that Sherry and I had was on a Sunday morning: we went to church. (I thought that was real spiritual.) A few weeks later, however, we were out very late on Saturday night. The next morning we went to church but ended up sleeping through the message. The week after that, we slept in on Sunday morning because of another late night. After a few weeks like this we knew something had to go, and it was those late Saturday nights. Our friends really thought that we were weird because we went to bed early, but that was okay with us. God was teaching us to keep our worshiping with the Body of Christ as a higher priority than our own fun and games.

We, as younger members of the Body of Christ, desperately need to recognize our position in and our relationship to the rest of the Body. As Peter writes, "Likewise you that are younger be subject to the elders" (1 Peter 5:5a). Peter also wrote Timothy, "Let no one despise your youth, but set the believers an example in speech and conduct, in love, in faith, in purity. Till I come, attend to the public reading of scripture, to preaching, to teaching" (1 Timothy 4:12, 13).

As younger members of the Body of Christ, we need the instruction, guidance, and discipline in the local church composed of older brothers and sisters, even if they are slower, quieter, or less emotional. It has taken me about ten years to even begin to understand the importance of this, and yet it needs to be heard: "... and all the more as you see the Day drawing near." It is far too easy for us to forget that to keep the Sabbath is one of the Commandments. May God help us be true to His Word and to live by the priorities set forth therein.

Priority Five: Ministry

> For we are his workmanship, created in Christ Jesus
> for good works, which God created beforehand, that
> we should walk in them.

Ephesians 2:10

In a youth group situation there are three different
kinds of boy-girl combinations; one group is the active
one that interacts with others and who is willing and
eager to take leadership responsibilities and who makes
things happen; the second group withdraws into themselves and takes a back seat, spectator position. This
group watches things happen. And the third group totally drops out, and they wonder what happened. Unfortunately, that "special someone" can steal our interests and zeal for ministry. If this happens, we fall into
the second or third group in a hurry.

Kent had a great ministry of music in our praise
meetings. He played guitar, sang and was used in a vital
way in the overall youth ministry. He began dating a
girl, and before too long he became irregular in his
attendance. After a month I wasn't seeing him at all,
and others were wondering what the problem was. I
wanted to call him and encourage him but the Spirit
said *no.*

One night I was in prayer for Kent, and God said,
"Now call him." So I did.

"Hey, this is Fred. How are you doing?"

"Oh, wow! This is unreal. I was just thinking of calling
you. I've been through a lot with a girl, but I guess I had

to learn the hard way. I should have known better than to date a non-Christian, and the whole thing was just not good for me at all. I started out with the idea of witnessing to her but I found no matter how I tried, she was having a negative influence on me. But anyway, what did you want?"

"Well, brother, I was praying for you, and God said to call. I was wondering if you would play the guitar and lead our singing Tuesday night."

"Wow, Fred, that sounds great. I've really missed it."

Kent was at the praise meeting that Tuesday, but it was to take him a few more weeks to rekindle the gift within him that he had left dormant. He learned the hard way that a relationship that steals the greater priority of ministry is not healthy. I knew right away, when he let the ministry that God had given him slide, that there was a problem with his girl friend.

In contrast to this, Dick and Jane worked in Campus Life during the week and taught a Sunday-school class on weekends. Their friendship certainly encouraged their ministries. Ministry needs to be protected, and any relationship that hinders one's ministry is more harmful than it is helpful.

Priority Six: Dating

Do not rebuke an older man but exhort him as you would a father; treat younger men like brothers, older women like mothers, younger women like sisters, in all purity.

1 Timothy 5:1, 2

Once God, family, school, job, Christians, and ministry are all in higher priority, we can start thinking about
dating. When all these areas have their divine position,
dating can have a positive effect in our lives. Sally and
Brooks have been living out these priorities in a beautiful way. Let's take a look at how it's done.

They are both reading, memorizing and meditating
on Scripture. Neither Sally nor Brooks have the greatest history of Bible reading, but now they are holding
each other to at least two chapters a night. They have
agreed that if they want to talk with each other the next
day, they'll read it. It's amazing what this commitment
has done to their devotional lives.

Their relationships with both parents have improved
since they have been dating one another. Both sets of
parents approve of their going out with one another
even though neither pair of parents is Christian. They
each spend an evening sitting home with their parents
on a regular basis. One weekend when Sally was away
looking at colleges Brooks went over to spend the night
just talking with Sally's mother, and she loved it!

They have respect for the time that their school work
and jobs require. Since this is their senior year, they
need to do well in school for future plans of college. On
the first report card Brooks got after dating Sally he got
four *A*'s and one *B*. Sally did equally well.

They have by no means isolated themselves from the
other Christians. They are regular in attending all
church-related meetings. Sally meets on Monday nights
with a small group of high-school girls and is teaching
them principles of the Christian life. Most of these girls

have been Christians for under one year and this meeting is a tremendous source of growth for them.

Also, they are both active in spreading the Gospel in their high schools. Brooks told almost everyone on his football team the Gospel of the Love of Jesus and goes out weekly to share Jesus with others. One night a week both Sally and Brooks go out to visit old friends with the idea in mind of ministering to them in some way.

Not long ago Sally said one of the greatest things anyone could say about a boy-girl relationship: "Brooks encourages me to be all that God wants me to be." That has to be the ultimate statement about any relationship. That's just not human, it's godly, and it's beautiful.

After all we have discussed, you might be anxiously asking, "Now am I ready to date?" Fortunately, I don't have to answer that question. In fact, I can't. You, and only you, have to ". . . work out your own salvation with fear and trembling" (Philippians 2:12). However, as you become more of a follower of our Lord, I pray that you will be obedient to Jesus as you ask Him that question.